The Hidden Qua

# The Hidden Qualities of Water

Edited by Wolfram Schwenk

Floris Books

First published as individual articles as noted
at the end of each chapter.

This one-volume edition first published
by Floris Books, Edinburgh, in 2007.

British Library CIP Data available

ISBN 978-086315-610-6

Printed in Great Britain
by Bell & Bain, Glasgow

# Contents

# Introduction

Water quality is measured in the modern world by the standard of what substances are absent or present in it, whether dissolved or in suspension. Water qualifies as drinking water when it is free of illness-causing bacteria, poisonous and foul smelling impurities, and when it does not corrode piping. These are necessary requirements, but in fact are not really sufficient to characterize water fit for drinking.

Many people sense that the question of water quality cannot be adequately met simply by considering prescriptive limits on undesirable impurities. Within our human experience, we know how water can be refreshing and enlivening, and we recognize, too, when these characteristics are missing. Could such sense perceptions be scientifically captured and described? Is there a scientific approach which could define the properties of good water over and beyond the absence of unwanted constituents? Doesn't the quality of mobility in water, without which it cannot fulfil its life-promoting activities, have a role to play here?

Theodor Schwenk (1910–86), author of *Sensitive Chaos* and founder of the Institute of Flow Sciences in Herrischried, in the southern Black Forest region of Germany, as well as his successors, have endeavoured to explore answers to these questions. Using the drop picture method developed at the Institute to research the flow behaviour of water, they have opened up the way towards throwing encouraging light on the above issues.

The first English collection of the Institute's publications, entitled *Water — The Element of Life* (1989) has long been out of print. Wilkens' *Understanding Water*, published in 2005, gave a brief overview of the research work of the Herrischried scientists, while in the present volume we explore certain aspects of their work in more depth. These writings show clearly that the results attained have been only achievable thanks to an unconventional, yet consciously and scientifically transparent, approach. This very approach, particularly in the light of today's global water problems, also needs to be discussed.

Effective water management will be one of the decisive challenges of the twenty-first century. Frontline causes for this are, amongst others, lack of clean water in dry regions which through mismanagement, climate change and population growth is becoming ever more threatening; and widespread disregard in developed countries for the natural quality of water resources. Ultimately the root of this neglect lies in ethical deficits which pervade today's scientific thinking, and in the resulting behaviour of humans in relation to nature and their fellow human beings. These deficits are already apparent in the research process itself, in its reductionist procedures which unconsciously foster a depreciation of nature. Starting with the very basis of scientific methodology, we must break out of such reductionism and learn to study real living phenomena to the extent that we can comprehend them in ways that are appropriate to their specific qualities. In water research, this means a type of attentiveness which can be acquired through a suitably fluid way of thinking. Such an in-depth appreciation of the research subject should form the beginning of a new environmental ethic — a path which at the same time would open up new ways of thinking. The task of learning to understand water, together with related questions regarding its life-sustaining properties, needs such an approach.

Just as it is necessary in sustainable agriculture to allow plants and animals a biologically appropriate life, water too needs an approach appropriate to its nature as a liquid, not only in how it is treated but also in how it is conceived. Science itself needs to develop and practise a conceptual approach adapted specifically to the nature of the research subject itself.

Today's prevailing paradigms and conceptual modelling for natural sciences have been established through experience of the world of solid bodies, and for this world they are appropriate. However, in the world of fluid bodies they are no longer suitable. Here, the scientific basis for establishing an appropriate cognitive approach is largely missing. Step by step this has to be developed and tested.

An old, tried and tested expression goes: 'It takes a thief to know a thief,' meaning, 'like recognizes like.' In order to perceive truly the object of one's research, it is necessary to inwardly connect with the subject and in empathy assimilate its character. One must make oneself compatible. The behavioural study of animals in the wild — whether monkeys, dolphins, penguins or migrating birds — has registered impressive successes based on this principle. Equally, should we want to tackle successfully the questions and tasks that water poses us, we need an appropriately fluid thinking for the scientific and practical management of water. The world of fluids is less contoured and more transient than that of solids. It is a world of ceaseless metamorphosis and thus far more difficult to grasp. The physical condition of fluids is more like an event or behaviour than a state. What occurs as a stable state for solid bodies, appears in fluids as a process, which carries on remaining a process. A language is therefore needed to represent fluid phenomena, a language that characterizes rather than defines, in a particularly careful and meticulous way. To practise this is the special challenge of water research. Our research group in Herrischried takes great care to undertake this task consciously in their research into the creative processes within water flow. Where the typical reductionist scientific methodology of today simply passes by, real attentiveness and awareness are required towards water phenomena and how they originate. The researcher who practises this gradually acquires a new mentality in regard to water, permeated by awareness and appreciation, not, as typically elsewhere, concerned with assessing water against one or other application as a utility (see for instance, Delli Priscoli, *et al.* 2004). Water ethics begin with the question: 'With what sort of mindset do I approach water? With what mindset can I observe its nature adequately as a scientist?' These questions and the quest for human empathy with liquid water lie behind all the individual research projects in the Institute of Flow

Sciences. Both in content and in method, the way forward must be set down with these first steps — and this does not happen by itself. We have communicated and reported in many publications on this approach and the regenerative impulses that arise from it. The present collection of writings is a representative selection translated into English.

Most of these articles deal, from one angle or another, with the creative processes in water and the astonishing and mysterious fact that in liquid water — which appears to be ideally formless with regard to its material characteristics — formative processes occur through manifold sequences of movement within a body of water. How and under what conditions these occur, and how such creative processes make visible aspects of the mobility of water — one of the biologically decisive properties of water — can best be methodically shown with the drop picture method, which is discussed in the middle of the book. The concluding Summary gathers in a condensed form the fundamental results of the work. In wider terms, discussion of the path of research, and the individual steps of the scientific-ethical task of acquiring a conceptual mindset appropriate for the behaviour of fluids, can be found in the remaining articles. Acknowledgments are due here for the fundamental contribution to this approach arising from Rudolf Steiner's spiritual science.

Working with the drop picture method has proven itself as a valuable educational tool in the pursuit of an appropriate mindset for exploring fluid nature. The aim of this exploration is on one hand to give water the opportunity of expressing itself under varying conditions, so that it can be observed in relation to those variables; and on the other hand to allow water samples to express themselves under selected and exactly identical conditions, so that their individual characters may be subject to comparison. Through this process, we become aware that we are dealing with natural laws, which are close and analogous to living nature, and in fact are perhaps themselves the very foundation of living nature. As a result, one starts to discover evidence of the life-serving functions of water.

In the introductory articles, our exploration, angled from many sides, is steered towards the role of water in life, water's functions in the whole earth organism, water's character as a fluid, the relationship between creative processes in moving water and the emergence of life, as well as, finally, the conscious attitudes of people in relation to water. Against this background, articles 4 to 9 describe research work with the drop picture method. The final contribution attempts an overview of the formative conditions in living things as reflected in the above-mentioned creative processes. Within lies a key as to why organic life needs water in order to be able to sustain itself in physical matter. A Summary section gives some of the research results summarized as a kind of abstract.

The Institute of Flow Sciences, where this body of work has taken place, is a small private research body which undertakes its tasks with very limited financial means funded by voluntary donations and without state support. The Institute needs further support. Otherwise, with only limited financial and staff capacity, the Institute may not be able to respond to initiatives and interest arising from the reading of this book.

Wolfram Schwenk, 2007

THEODOR SCHWENK

# 1. What is Living Water?

Those who keep up with developments in current water issues may frequently come across references to 'living water' and 'dead water.' For some, these are perfectly familiar terms and concepts they use every day in their professional practice. Others reject them on the ground that since water possesses none of the characteristics of living organisms, it cannot be spoken of as either alive or dead.

City dwellers who go into the mountains and have the chance to drink from a bubbling spring in some high meadow, know at first hand what living water is. Precisely because they come from a city background, they really can distinguish between dead and living water. They know, of course, that city water has to meet strict hygiene standards. But they have had personal experience of the vast difference between that water and what they drink from a mountain spring. And though what comes out of city taps can be reliably counted on not to contain coliform bacteria or other toxic organisms and is sure to be free of nitrates and phosphates, do these criteria suffice when it comes to characterizing what they have experienced as living water?

In dealing with modern water problems, the inevitable question arises of how to describe and verbalize the concepts of living and dead water — looking beyond immediate experience and the familiarity of those terms.

We will try to work out such a concept in the following pages.

Let us begin by recalling some unspoiled brook that we may have seen making its way through the depths of some forest, now burbling over pebbly stretches, now pent up in quiet pools. It sparkles in the changing play of light that breaks through the screen of foliage above;

it leaps ahead in rippling wavelets, alternating between soft murmuring and silvery tinkling. It takes a meandering course among the trees, twisting this way and that as though to make its lively game last longer. Surely this water cannot be called anything but living!

If we pick up a stone along the bank, its wet underside and the hole it came from will be found alive with tiny wriggling creatures. Should water that contains such life be designated 'living'? We certainly do not want the water that comes out of our taps to be full of such life-forms, even though their presence is considered by science to be one of the best indicators of a water's excellence, and scientific classifications are actually based on the presence or absence of that life.

Nevertheless, none of this is welcome in our drinking water, whether it comes out of taps or from mountain springs. The concept of 'living water' must be based on some other sort of criteria.

What is it that attracts us so powerfully to living water? Do we perhaps feel that water flowing out of taps in sunless city apartment blocks is dead and almost unreal because of imponderable elements in the environment? Whereas water that constantly pours out of a spring in the middle of a flower-filled mountain meadow, sparkling in the pure, cold air and in light reflected from shimmering snow peaks round about, perfectly satisfies our concept of what living water is.

Our age is drawn to articulating human experiences of the most deeply felt and lived. So too in the case of living water, which we want to grasp in the sense of both understanding what it is and how to have it and hold on to it.

But if we literally try to take hold of water, it slips through our fingers and flows away unless we put it in some sort of container. If the container is solid we can 'catch' water in it; then it quietens down immediately. However, this means that it is already well on the way to being dead, to losing the quality that originally made it living water. And the concepts that we form of it suffer the same fate: the moment one tries to capture the true nature of water in a hard and fast definition, the reality of it is no longer there. To be adequate, concepts of water must retain something of water's liveliness and movement, of the way it lends itself to constant change. They must be capable of metamorphosis, shaped in harmony with, and able to express, water's functions.

If we ask again at this point: 'What, specifically, is living water?' we see that another question has to be answered first, namely: 'What is life?'

Life manifests itself in quite specific, tangible attributes in every living creature: in growth, reproduction, metamorphosis (that is, changes of form that take place in organisms); in metabolic functions, which include the digesting of food and excreting of wastes; in the regulation of chemical, warmth and other processes; in phases of growth and fading that rise and fall in definite time patterns, always subject to life's characteristic rhythms.

Are these attributes of life to be found in water? Does water grow? Can it reproduce? We certainly know water to be the very prototype of everything formless and fluid; how, then, could it possibly be said to undergo metamorphosis, to change its form, as living organisms do? Is it subject to digestive and excretory processes? Does it possess definite organs that perform typical organ functions? Can it adapt itself to fixed determining factors? Does water evolve into an organism and then die? Are autonomous rhythms, such as the heartbeat of an animal, to be found in water?

The answer to all these questions is of course obvious: water possesses none of these characteristics of living organisms. Whatever it turns out to be, we feel sure that it must rank lower than a living creature.

But if that is so, must our search for an adequate definition of living water not end up in a blind alley?

It would seem so. Yet what of the experience of people who work professionally with water and daily apply the concept 'dead' and 'living' water in their practice? Perhaps we had better wait to draw conclusions until we have looked at the problem from another angle.

Everyone knows that water has a close affinity with all forms of life. So we may ask what the connection is — whether manifestations of life can occur in the absence of water. Is growth possible without it? Propagation? Metamorphosis? Are digestion and excretion conceivable where water is lacking? Isn't water essential to conversion processes and organ functions? Is it not the great mediator and regulator of chemical, warmth and other processes, both in living organisms and outside them? Can a living organism even come into being without water's help? And, in the last analysis, could rhythm exist in organisms if there were no fluids?

Here again, to put the question is to find that the answer is self-evident: none of the above life-characteristics would be present without water. Life depends on water for its very life! Again we are confronted by a riddle: water does not manifest a single life-characteristic. Yet where water is lacking, there can be no life. All the factors noted depend upon water.

At this point the ground beneath our feet begins to seem somewhat less than solid, as can often happen with true riddles. But isn't it perfectly natural to feel at sea when pursuing the theme of water? Perhaps this state of affairs may even prove an asset and set us on the right course for our inquiry.

How, then, does water, which has no life-characteristics of its own, provide the very basis of life in all its various manifestations? Water embraces everything, exists in and throughout everything; because it rises above the distinctions between plants and animals and human beings; because it is a universal element shared by all; itself undetermined, yet determining; because, like the primal mother it is, it supplies the stuff of life to everything living.

And what makes water capable of all these feats? — the following aspects:

❖ renouncing any form of its own, it becomes the creative matrix for form in everything else;

❖ renouncing any life of its own, it becomes the primal substance of all life;

❖ renouncing material stability, it becomes the implementer of material change;

❖ renouncing any rhythm of its own, it becomes the progenitor of rhythm elsewhere.

Is it any wonder, then, that in all highly developed cultures, water has always been held sacred as a magically transforming substance, as the very 'water of life'?

Now that we have considered the plant, animal, and human kingdoms as specimens of living organisms, let us try to come closer to answering to our question by bringing that all-inclusive living being, the Earth-organism, into the picture.

We find a number of comprehensive descriptions of the Earth as a living entity, in which it is shown that such a concept is no mere theory, but a reality apprehensible in human experience. These studies range from works by the great astronomer Johannes Kepler to contemporary descriptions by Guenther Wachsmuth, Walther Cloos and others.[1]

Contemplating this vast living organism Earth, one's attention is drawn again and again to the layered structure of its great enveloping mantles and to the rhythms that play in and through them. A glance at the surface of the Earth reminds us, for example, that 70% of it is covered by water. This watery surface, in its immense extension, provides a plane of contact with the atmosphere. Here an exchange sets in between the elements of air and water that moves in both directions, up and down. Thus, water is absorbed into the atmosphere, where it works as the great regulator in matters of climate and in meteorological processes and their rhythms. Meteorologists, whose daily observation of the weather and its changes gives them a special sense, shared by all outdoors people, for what goes on in the atmosphere, often find that they have to speak of processes there as if they were something living. August Schmauss, for example, talks of 'biological concepts in meteorology,' of an 'orchestral score' of atmospheric happenings, with 'entrances' in the annual pattern of the unfolding seasons.[2] Paul Raethjen says in his treatise on the dynamics of cyclones that 'the atmosphere behaves like a living creature,' and elsewhere in the same work we read:

> For one thing, cyclones have a metabolic process without which they could not exist: they constantly draw new masses of air into their vortices and excrete other masses in their outward-spirallings. Then too, . . . they have a typical life history with characteristic beginning, developing, and aging phases. They reproduce themselves, not in a wave-like spreading out in space, but like a living creature, in the sense that a young 'frontal cyclone' is born out of the womb of an adult 'central cyclone.'[3]

We know that cyclones (low-pressure areas) have to do with water. A 'low' and rain belong in the same concept.

Thus, the life of the earth-organism as a whole is just as closely bound up with water as the life of any of the creatures on it. Rhythmic processes are present in the cosmos that play into the various atmospheric strata, giving rise to the rhythms found wherever water is. Rudolf Steiner, Guenther Wachsmuth, Ernst Marti, George Adams, Hermann Poppelbaum, Lili Kolisko and others have acquainted us with these 'formative forces' raying in from the cosmos; they have taught us to distinguish between them and to recognize how they build and shape all Earth's living organisms.

Everything in nature forms one indivisible fabric woven out of living interchange. An all-encompassing world of life comes into being from the interplay of cosmic peripheral forces, meteorological forces, forces of the elements, the Earth, and all its living organisms.

A great deal of evidence has already been uncovered showing that the Earth, and the varied life-forms on it, function in harmony with universal processes, and every year more and more evidence for this is reported. Almost every natural rhythm is based on water's mediation, from moon cycles reflected in the hydrosphere and planetary cycles known to meteorology, right down to the innumerable physiological rhythms found in every living organism. For example, woodcutters in the forests of Brazil still set the price of the wood they fell by the date of its cutting, that is, by the moon phase, because its water content (and thus its keeping quality) depends on these cosmic influences. The patterns of movement that planets weave in space are also reflected in the structure of the various plant families: thus, for example, the Venus pattern appears in the regular pentagram common to all rose plants. If it were not for the mediating role that water plays, these formative forces could not work their way into terrestrial patterns. In the tides, the seas are caught up in the swing of cosmic rhythms which they then transmit to the Earth and its creatures. All movement in water is affected by cosmic formative forces and serves the function of transmitting them.[4]

Thus, water occupies a mediating position between Earth and the universe, and is the port of entry through which cosmic-peripheral forces pass into the earth realm.

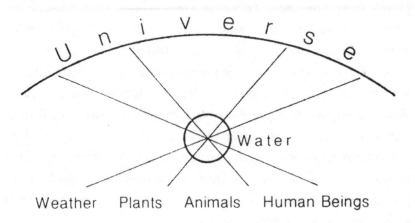

May we not call water 'nature's central organ,' its 'heart,' the pulsing, oscillating drop that lets the whole cosmos pass through it? Its functions make it indeed the primal organ; it transmits cosmic forces and activities into the earth just as the heart mediates between processes of the upper and lower parts of the organism and — functionally speaking — embraces all the other organs.

Water does not grow because it is itself growth, growth-as-function, growth uncommitted to any particular growth pattern. It is not subject to metamorphosis because it is itself the universal element of change that runs through every possible form without becoming fixed in any. While not itself subject to regulation, it serves as nature's regulator in numberless instances. Though it possesses no organs of its own, it is itself the primal organ jointly shared by everything that lives — an organ that remains at the functional level rather than presses on to the physical-organic stage. None of life's attributes come to outward expression in water, but they are all functionally present in it in the form of possibility, capacity, and action.

What intelligence we find built into humankind and nature! — such as the provision that controls warmth in the bloodstream and keeps the normal body temperature level at a constant 37°C (98.6°F). Even a slight deviation from that temperature spells illness. How intelligently, then, has nature arranged that water's lowest specific heat coincides with a temperature of exactly 37°, and therefore absorbs warmth most rapidly at that temperature!

But water possesses many qualities beyond those singled out here for mention, and these enable it to be the matrix of all living things. What a composition of wisdom every living organism is, each single facet of it revealing new marvels! And water is wisdom's very element, the focus in which wisdom is concentrated and out of which its activity flows into the greatest and the least of living things. Indeed, it is because life is wisdom and water wisdom's element that there can be such a thing as the water of life.

Now that we have come to know water as the functional compendium of all outer forms of life, let us look from this new angle at some of the life-attributes discussed above.

Take nutrition, for example. Not only is the movement of food-stuffs through the organism unthinkable without the help of water but almost all chemical and other changes depend on water. Drinking water of a quality that meets health requirements holds the balance between alkalinity and acidity.

Water, of course, occurs in greater volume in the ocean than anywhere else in nature. The composition of seawater is almost identical with that of blood, the only difference being that seawater contains magnesium where human blood contains iron — a fact that must be looked at in relation to the needs of air-breathing organisms.

What can be observed as the growth-process in trees, for example, is present in water as pure function. Moving water consists of layers that continually flow past one another at varying speeds. We find the same thing happening in the tree's cambium layer, where growth takes place. There too, newly formed cells slip past the old ones in an outward flow that widens the cambium ring without splitting it.

The vortex is the functional pattern of all the metamorphoses and shaping found in water. When layers flowing at different speeds pass one another, a process of deflection and rolling-up takes place, and this leads to the formation of a vortex. We find the same thing happening wherever contingent growth-speeds vary in an organism. An example is the way a stem or leaf bends and starts to roll up when one side grows faster than the layer next to it.

Organs are also built on the model of the vortex-forming process, as may be noted in the way they always create a boundary between an inner and an outer space.

Reproduction, in the sense of repetition, is everywhere to be found in water, again of course at the functional level. Trains of vortices are an example. Here we see a process similar to the spawning of daughter-cyclones in a water-saturated atmosphere as described above by Paul Raethjen.

As for the phenomenon of rhythm, water must be called its very element. The word 'rhythm' is derived from the Greek verb 'to flow.'

And water does indeed flow rhythmically. This can be seen in the
rhythmic pattern of waves and meandering watercourses, just as it
can be heard in the audible rhythms of brooks and oceans. Numerical
relationships found in physiological rhythms appear again in phenomena of air and water. Sound, for example, travels four times as
fast through seawater as it does through air. This same proportion is
found again in the rhythmic processes of man's fluid and airy organisms in the 4:1 pulse-breathing rate.

Such facts make it evident how profoundly related water is to all
life-functions, and most especially to those in the human organism.

Many of water's qualities also show a distinct relationship to soul
and spiritual attributes in human beings. Not only does water serve
the cause of bodily life, but also that of the inner man in that, for
example, the brain floats in water and is thus relieved of the pull of
gravity. Physiologically speaking, this is what makes thinking possible.

Certain descriptions of water can equally well be applied to soul
capacities; we speak of the power to cleanse, to purify, to heal, and
both water and the soul are referred to as 'in balance,' 'clear,' 'reflective,' 'refreshing.' And just as healthy souls refrain from going to
extremes, so water holds a balance between extremes of heavy and
light with its buoyancy, between alkaline and acid, between warmth
and cold, and — with its rainbow colours — between light and dark.
And because it is so balanced an element it has the capacity to regulate, to heal, to create a mobile, living equilibrium. But when water
comes into a resting state of balance, it stagnates, loses its 'life,' is as
though paralyzed.

Since water is universal and a stranger to one-sidedness, it is the
means whereby the full range of life is made possible. Hence, it is
truly the 'water of life.' The concept 'water' might best be expressed
as 'universality through renunciation,' 'wisdom's element.' Because
of the wisdom that makes it what it is, it is fitted to be the carrier of
cosmic forces.

What, then, is living water?

It is water that contains not only the cosmic elements radiating life into the earth sphere, but that also has an inherent relationship to man as body, soul, and spirit.

Today this may sound like anthropomorphism. But there is a practical aspect to the statement. As we contemplate the civilization of our time, we can be aware of its water problems, but also of the direction we must take to solve them. If water is deprived of its universal nature by becoming tainted with substances like salts and detergents, it cannot maintain its universal function and continue to be the transmitter of nature's living wisdom. Wholesome water is water that maintains itself in active balance. But how far the sewage-laden rivers of today are from such a definition! They can no longer be recipients of cosmic forces. In many cases, indeed, the opposite is true: they can only be called 'chemical infernos, veritable hells.'

If we are to solve the water problems facing us today — and this includes such technical measures as must be taken — there is no other path open to us than to rediscover water's cosmic aspect. And this calls for nothing less than a new sense for what life is. From now on, everything depends on our developing what one professional in the field of water sanitation recently described as 'water-consciousness.' But that means recognizing that water is the carrier of cosmic energies and understanding how it can be rehabilitated to become once again their carrier.

Does this provide us with a concept of what living water is? We have come to know it as the bearer of wisdom, as the instrument of cosmic forces and orderings, in short, of life. We have found it to be living nature's primary organ, through which everything alive must pass.

While the work of our Institute takes its motivation from the restorative impulse vital to the solution of our time's great problems, it seeks that solution through grasping the true nature of water, seeks it, one might say, in a supersensible water-consciousness intent on taking the spirit of nature as the guide of its science and technology.

**Notes**

1. Johannes Kepler (1571–1630), German astronomer who discovered Kepler's laws of planetary motion. Postulated ray theory of light to explain vision. See Guenther Wachsmuth (1932), also Walther Cloos (1977).
2. See August Schmauss (1945).
3. See Paul Raethjen (1953).
4. See Theodor Schwenk (1967, 1976, 1988); also A. Wilkens, M. Jacobi & W. Schwenk (2005).

First published in German as 'Zum Begriff des lebendigen Wassers,' in Theodor Schwenk, *Das Wasser, Herausforderung an das moderne Bewußtsein,* Herrischried 1985. Translated by Marjorie Spock, first published in English in *The Golden Blade* 1969.

Theodor Schwenk

# 2. The Nature of Water

The essence of a thing is never revealed to us directly. As Goethe said, we should aim at letting nature's underlying patterns speak to us through an object's essence and being. Then the events and activity we perceive can be used like writing, which we can learn to read in order to capture something of the essence and being of the object itself. To experience the essence and being of water in nature, therefore, it is necessary to take in its actions and perceive them as writing or a language. One must learn to read this language, practising until the letters disappear and the meaning, the essence of what is perceived, surfaces.

It is clear that even when we have clarified certain aspects of water as a substance, we have not yet found our way towards water as an element. Those individual aspects are like grains of sand on the shore, that is to say comparable with the properties of a solid: density, incompressibility, viscosity, power of dissolving, heat capacity, conductivity, anomalies in density, heat of melting and evaporation, freezing point, dielectric coefficients, and so on.

Physics describes each of these properties separately, defines constants, and where interrelations are needed they are given as formulae instead of spiritual connections. Thus a technical mastery of water is gained, but at the same time we lose our connection with the essence and being of water.

In consideration of this, we must ask: what can we observe in our universe as a consequence of water having, for example, particular heat properties? Let us look at this question in terms of three important heat properties: specific heat, heat of melting and heat of evaporation. What occurs through these three properties?

*1. Specific heat:* this expresses how much heat is needed, for example, to warm 1 kg of water by 1°C. The answer is one kilocalorie (Cal). Compared to other substances, this value is very high. A lot of heat is needed to get an increase in temperature in water. Naturally, such inertia means that large bodies of water need long, continuous, intense heat before their temperature increases. Consequently, oceans, lakes and large rivers have a relatively constant temperature, which is maintained and regulated. A certain inertia is a prerequisite for stability, reflecting a number of constant conditions.

Because the big water masses of the world have a fairly stable temperature, both the extremes of summer and winter are made more temperate, this moderating effect increasing with the difference in temperature between the water and the air. This is because large movements, such as ocean currents, convey warmth to areas that are less warm. Logically, because of the large heat absorption potential of water (the high specific heat), enormous quantities of heat are transported when a water mass flows from the equatorial region towards the north. This quantity of warmth is defined by water's high specific heat. The fact that higher latitudes receive so much warmth to moderate their cold climate, effectively making those zones habitable, is simply due therefore to the constant of the specific heat of water.

Wind and air currents are also set in motion, through which evaporated water is distributed around the planet. Evaporation is the 'motor' of meteorological events and thereby of the distribution of rainfall.

The specific heat of water is dependent on temperature. At different temperatures, water requires different amounts of heat to be warmed through 1°C. The minimum is at 37°C, at which point the least amount of heat is necessary to warm water through 1°C. Isn't nature here pointing a finger at the temperature regulation of the human organism?

*2. Latent heat of melting (80 Cal/kg):* compared to other substances, the heat of melting of water is again an extreme value. To convert

1 kg of ice into liquid water, both at 0°C, 80 kilocalories (Cal) are required. The opposite is naturally also true, to convert 1 kg of water into ice, both at 0°C, the same amount of heat is released. This has consequences which can be clearly explained.

An abrupt drop in temperature in lakes and the ocean is prevented by the high heat of melting of water. A large amount of heat also needs to be extracted at the freezing point, in order for water to freeze. When it does freeze, this large amount of heat is released which benefits the water and surrounding air, significantly slowing the freezing process. Ocean temperatures are consequently kept at a relatively constant temperature, and a kind of medium warmth zone is established which is very stable.

In addition, during freezing an ice skin is created which, for example in northern areas, protects against further freezing. The heat of melting is again an excellent method of regulating constancy, a constancy almost like that of a living organism.

3. *Latent heat of evaporation (540 Cal/kg):* this also expresses itself in a very high value: 540 kilocalories (Cal) are necessary to convert 1 kg of water into 1 kg of vapour, both at a temperature of 100°C. This has the effect of preventing the air from becoming too hot, as water has the capacity of taking up enormous quantities of heat before it evaporates. When the air is too cold, the condensing water releases heat back to the air. This results in an unimaginably extensive regulation of air temperatures and moderation of climatic extremes. The warmer the air becomes, the more evaporation it can hold, and the longer the temperature can be held constant. Again we here have a self-regulation capacity in nature, based on the latent heat of evaporation. These regulatory properties function along the same lines as those previously discussed, with particular relevance to the boundary between water and air.

These three heat properties can then be seen as activating the maintenance of balance in the three zones of the Earth:

a) Due to its high latent heat of melting, that is, because water releases a lot of heat before it freezes, the polar zones are shifted to higher latitudes, much further than would be the case with a lesser latent heat.

b) Correspondingly, through the high latent heat of evaporation — because evaporating water extracts such immense quantities of heat from the air — the hot zone is moderated and pushed back towards the equator.

c) The specific heat reveals itself as a highly effective temperature regulator in the temperate zone at the level required for the liquid state of water between freezing and evaporating.

Now, what occurs through the interaction of these three properties? A living space is created: the temperate zone is enlarged, extended to the north and to the south. Here the life of organisms, the earth, the oceans and the atmosphere can develop to an optimum and thus conditions are established for human activities.

Through temperature regulation, water shows itself to be the classic regulatory contributor to a state of balance. In fact, all other functions of water can be considered in terms of its supremely intelligent capability of regulation.

The world of living organisms is made possible at all thanks to these properties of water. When one considers that these are the properties which underlie life processes for all living creatures — in their internal bodies, their environments and for the earth itself — the following question comes to the fore: do not such events deserve to be observed in terms of life itself instead of, as up to now, physio-chemical data framing the observation of life?

Let's take a quick look at some other characteristics of life. In all living things, the following are to be found: growth, reproduction, regeneration, substance conversions and metamorphoses, nutrition and elimination, targeted processes, own rhythms, developing and passing away, tropisms, sense capacities, and so on. Not one of these factors can function without water, and the appropriateness of water for each factor provides an optimum set of conditions for life.

When we consider water for life in relation to three aspects of the human organism — metabolism, sensory organs and rhythmical activities — we find that water is already predisposed towards such processes. In fact, one can say that the very character of the human organism is to be found within the fluid processes of water.

Where water occurs, we have the conditions for organisms to be present: water is, as it were, *the* process organism of nature. The water bodies of the world — whether stream, lake, ocean or the atmosphere itself — can be seen as not yet limited, open organisms functioning on the level of flow processes. They can all be considered under the aspects of metabolic, rhythmic and sensorial functions, building towards a higher unity: the very foundation of the life-body of the earth. The earth is also connected through its liquid corpus — like human beings — to the cosmos.

Having looked at water as a milieu for life, at water within organisms and at water as a process organism in itself, as it appears to us in streams, lakes and the sea, let us now take another look at the character of water in itself. No property of life is possible without water. This means, all properties of life come together in water, intersecting as if at a critical point of equilibrium. A few examples can illustrate this:

1. In chemistry, the pH of water lies exactly between alkaline and acidic.

2. The interplay between light and dark is observed in the primordial watery phenomenon of the rainbow.

3. In mechanics, water occupies a place between heavy and light; it counters heaviness with buoyancy.

4. In thermodynamics, the convection capacity (flowing heat) of water lies between heat conductivity, which particularly suits solid bodies, and heat radiation, the essence of which is light-like.

5. In relation to form, water has an intermediate position between lineal/central and peripheral circling universal forces, the result being a spiral, which is visible in every water vortex.

As a mediating presence in nature, water acts as the very interface, a hypomochlion (fulcrum), and so acts as a regulating element, as practically no other substance can.

We can observe these realities from the most diverse perspectives and so we can also say: all properties of life are assembled in water, as optima or maxima, and together they manifest in a unique composition — water.

No other element assumes such a central role, functioning in many ways like a heart organ within nature. Just as the heart mediates activities between lower and higher organizations in humans, so water mediates activities between the cosmic and earth worlds. Like the heart, too, water unites these activities in a whole. As such, water shows itself to be the first primordial organism, an image of flowing life itself, the 'blood of nature.'

Water takes on a particular character in each and every one of the manifold creations of nature. Each of these — a bird, a mouse, a wildflower, or a tree — can be seen as a particular and discrete development of the potential of water. Water comprehends all of them, it is what they all have in common, the fact that they all contain water. However, water contains every living organism as a process, as if it were the original, archetypal living organism. The life process itself is mirrored in its activity.

What wisdom we find already in the workings of the smallest organism, the tiniest organ, and what wisdom, too, do we discover underlying the whole environment of life! Water is the basis of both, and manifests itself as the carrier of this wisdom, as its focal point, in which it is collected and from which it acts in everything that lives. Water, in fact, appears in nature as flowing wisdom.

Should one want to express the idea of water in different terms, one could do so in the following style: wisdom surrenders itself to such an extent that it is captured in a material, yet is not fixed, remaining as a life process between spirit and material incarnation. We have already recognized water as an interface in nature *between* extremes, an intermediate space in which life is possible, as a middle which is not static but which is active and manifests itself in outward oscillations towards both extremes. Through this, a necessary eccentricity is created in nature, which maintains movement and does not let life become rigid. Through this, too, it is always rhythmic.

So we can broadly capture the idea of water: it constitutes not just the middle between spirit and material manifestation but mediates between both in rhythmical motion. It acts as the small eccentricity of nature and through this results in life. One can capture it at a small point, which yet has a tremendous effect.

First published in German as 'Vom Wesen des Wassers in der Natur,' in *Mitteilungen der Weleda AG*, Arlesheim und Schwäbisch Gmünd, 11, 1970. Translated by Jessica Read, slightly shortened.

WOLFRAM SCHWENK

# 3. Water, the Universal Element of Life

Of all the ways in which humans are bound to water, one has indisputable priority: water is the most vital and irreplaceable prerequisite for life.

There is however a deep rift between modern scientific thinking about water and the life-giving role it fulfils for humans, animals and plants. We therefore need to look at water with fresh eyes, and to reorientate our mode of questioning. How can we learn to understand the life-giving actions of water?

Water creates a problem of understanding for us in its very nature. On one hand it is the most important life substance for humans and every other living creature; on the other, seen purely as a material substance, it is a mineral. A chemist describes water as a fluid synthesis of hydrogen and oxygen gases. This apparent contradiction of a mineral representing the most important life substance leads to a scientific no-man's-land where no one really feels competent. Even in nutritional science textbooks the subject of water is more or less left out!

## *A threshold substance between animate and inanimate nature*

To begin with, we can make two observations. First, in early spring, before the buds have burst open, it may have been dry for a few weeks. The buds on the trees and shrubs are almost bursting with the sap almost set, but they still cannot open. Then overnight there comes a light drizzle, of a practically inconsequential amount. Just the slightest trace of moisture bathes the surface of the buds. The next morning they have opened, and the leaves have unrolled and unfurled.

So water makes growth possible, it leads to life.

Then we can see the very opposite happen. Following weeks of rain in late summer and autumn, the crops are still standing in the fields and cannot be harvested. They spoil and decompose because they are damp. Yet again, water comes into play, but in this case not leading to life, rather leading away from it, or perhaps we should rather say shifting to another form of life, where degradation, decomposition, disintegration and destruction take over.

In both cases, the contact of water with the surface of the plants was enough. From this, we can experience and learn that water is a threshold substance leading both to and from life. This shows us that we can understand nothing of water and its effects without examining it in the context where it is active. This is a vital characteristic which we will encounter again and again.

### Tasks within the organism

The mobility of water allows an organism to remain capable of growth, and within certain limits capable of metamorphosis, for its entire lifetime without becoming fixed and rigidified. Through water's high dissolving power, substances that are absorbed into the organism through nutrition or thereafter expelled, are continuously brought into new relationships with one another. This is not simply because they are dissolved but due also to the mobility and flow properties characteristic of water. Through these flows and movements, substances can arrive where they are needed within the organism or else can come to be expelled.

It is water which makes these relationships possible, first bringing them about and then also breaking them up. As a medium, a mediator of relationship, water is an instrument, a helper of the etheric body, which governs the task of organizing these relationships.

As an aside, it should be remembered that in relationship to heat, water exhibits several anomalies through which ideal life conditions for organisms are maintained and a life-friendly, balanced temperature regulation of the Earth organism is made possible (Kipp 1951, Schwenk 1985).

## *Freeing — leading into process — mediating relationships*

Water is capable of both freeing and bonding. Take for example a salt crystal, which is lying somewhere as a small cube and which has its own defined form, independent of its situation and environment. It might be lying next to a sugar crystal or other salt crystals, and they might even be touching each other: they remain next to one another, removed, as it were, from the flow of life and time. However, as soon as a little moisture is introduced, the crystals start to lose their contours, begin to melt and dissolve. Through the fluid which now binds them, the crystals interact with one another, and can even form new bonds. In place of the pre-existing forms, something new emerges, something that was not there before: the saltiness of the salt crystal, the sugariness of the sugar crystal, and so on. The dry crystal was not salty. Its saltiness, the active property with which it can take part in chemical processes, becomes manifest only once it is in solution. The ancient alchemists knew the maxim: *Corpora non agunt nisi soluta,* meaning, only when dissolved can substances have active effect. Through its power of dissolving, water opens and mediates the possibility of the dissolved substances coming into relationship with one another, and the possibility of new chemical bonds being formed or broken.

As a dry crystal, the salt was bounded by the small amount of space of its own volume. When dissolved in a jug of water, its substance stretches and spreads equally through the entire volume of the jug, losing its form while extending the space it occupies. 'Where there

is one body, there can be no second,' applies to the realm of solid
bodies. However, dissolved in water the same space can be taken up
together by more than one dissolved substance. Through dissolving,
water offers a way towards generalization, from which arise opportunities for further differentiations.

A body submerged in water loses the same weight as the water
it has displaced, thus becoming buoyant. This means that substances dissolved in water are held in suspension, they are freed
from gravity, water and substances in mutual support. The dry
form of a salt crystal is pulled by gravity towards the earth, and
so is totally orientated towards the earth. In a dissolved state, the
substance floats free of gravity, as if in outer space. There is no
longer just one direction in which physical forces can affect the
substance, now universal forces from all directions can affect the
substance equally. Only in this universal state — a fact which is
often not clearly enough recognized — can chemical processes
become active and interrelations between substances occur.

So we can say that: in the transition from solid to fluid, substances
become active, things move from a state to a process; everywhere in
nature where water is active and effective, we are involved with processes, not with static states.

Drawing this to a conclusion, I would therefore like to introduce
'renewal activity' to characterize the tasks of water. Further examples
of this will follow. For the time being we have seen how, thanks to
water's power of dissolving and bonding, the salt crystal has changed
its state and properties and opened up to new possibilities. These
activities which reveal themselves chemically are supported by physical activities, which express themselves particularly as flow movements; here, the renewal activity of water is directly observable as
a creative process. And in reality, every life process is connected to
creative processes.

## Water as an open system: without form, yet creating

Natural scientists these days, when discussing the creation of form, talk enthusiastically about self-organization in the physical world. The basis for morphology is sought in the theory of molecules and atoms of a particular substance. In the case of water, when left to itself, its form creation remains limited to spherical droplets. These can be observed, for example, hanging from a spider's web. Larger drops, however, whether hanging, lying on a surface or falling (depending on the surroundings), change and lose their spherical shape. Greater volumes of water with a free surface, for example in an open jug, orientate that open surface tangentially to the surface of the Earth, so recreating a section of the sphere of the Earth. Here the water surface is totally orientated to the Earth's circumference, and is no longer centred on a localized drop.

When external forces affect water and makes it move, new and varied forms are created, depending on surrounding conditions. In bodies of still water, wind can cause waves which travel over the surface. Stationary waves — forms which occur at a given point as long as water flows through it — are produced when constant flowing water encounters an obstacle. In this case, the wave-form and the substance which fills it are not bound to one another as in the case of solid bodies. Rather, the wave-form is constantly renewed thanks to the water which flows through in a 'steady flow balance' with the so-called stationary flow. The form of the stationary wave is itself created and maintained by movement and the continuous change of substance. The form-creating organization of the fluid does not result from the material in itself, but the fluid behaves rather as an open system, its organization resulting from interrelation with external factors.

Likewise, large stationary waves form an obstacle for oncoming flow, causing a succession of stationary capillary waves, as fine as hair, on the upstream side (see Fig.1).

**Figure 1.**  Stationary capillary waves in a stream with clean water (from Schwenk 1962)

Where these flow through and penetrate one another, a finely segmented honeycomb-like pattern of bumps and hollows is observable. The quantity and detail of these capillary waves depend on the properties of the water; this proves to be the modifying factor. The great diversity of flow shapes that we can observe in clean waters is conspicuously diminished in polluted waters (see Fig.2).

This indicates a connection between the degree of mobility of water, which enables form creation, and the quality of the water.

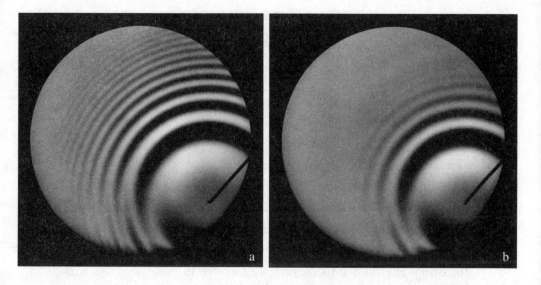

**Figure 2.** Capillary waves in pure and contaminated waters
(from Wilkens *et al.* 1995/2005)
2a. Clean water; numerous, fine capillary waves.
2b. Water contaminated with washing powder;
few, faded capillary waves.

This very connection is what we investigate with the drop picture method. Considered analytically, the diversity is dependent on the surface tension of the water. Should surface tension be reduced due to surface-active substances, for example from sewerage, only faded capillary waves occur.

In its encounter with the surrounding earth, water forms waves, not only upwards and downwards but also sideways — if one may refer to small meanders in this way. Even on steep slopes, it is seldom that water simply flows straight down. Generally, water engages with its surroundings in a winding, meandering fashion.

## *Organizing flow — organic formation movements*

From a distance, the tracing of tidal waters along a coast, such as the mudflats of a river at low tide (see Fig.3), gives the strong impression of an organic formation. In the flow patterns of water in sludge, observing what seem to be plant-like forms, we sense a conformity with a higher general organic order.

Exploring this further experimentally, we set up a large tray with a black bottom, filled with a few centimetres of syrup-like viscous liquid, on the surface of which white powder is spread. At one end of the tray a stick is dipped in and drawn through the liquid evenly and slowly; this brings the fluid into motion. Because of the viscosity, the stick only affects the area in the immediate vicinity. Further to the side the liquid is only weakly moved, and even further away the liquid remains still. The stick pulls some liquid with it, as a result of which patterns follow in its wake. Due to the powder, these become visible on the surface as fine bands. Slowly, the whole arrangement becomes unstable and starts to swing, as a result of which the further side areas are drawn into the moving fluid. Finally, there is a build-up of movement at the end of the tray, which leads to the development of a vortex pair (see Fig.4, left). Depending on our perception, here too the impression may arise of an organic

**Figure 3.**   Tidal flow at low tide in mudflats (from Schwenk 1962)

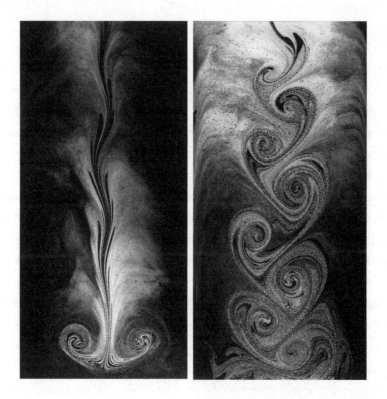

**Figure 4.**   Germlike and fully developed Karman Vortex Street,
chasing forms behind a stick drawn through a viscous
fluid; left high viscosity, right slightly more viscous than
water (Schwenk 1962).

form, something like a germinating plant. However, the impression is
general, without reference to any particular species.

Intensifying this process by using thinner, watery fluid, we find
that it is not only layering which occurs along the trace of the stick.
At an appropriate speed, the chasing vortex pair can no longer keep
up with the stick but becomes unstable and frees itself. It swings
alternately from left to right and is replaced by new chasing vortices.
The total result is called a Karman Vortex Street (see Fig.4, right).

The originally round spots of sprinkled powder are pulled into bands and filaments. Converging from different sides, they run together, tightly neighbouring yet without crossing through each other, and are caught by an inward rolling movement. This is a trace of the so-called shear flow which occurs through speed differences within the fluid, whereby gliding layers of the same speed result. These are not layers of different material. Rather, within the homogenous substance, what happens is that areas of equal speed glide next to areas of different speed, rolling into one another.

On the outside, such vortices have a very slow period of rotation. The nearer to the centre, the greater the angular velocity, and accordingly the period of rotation becomes ever shorter towards the centre (until just short of the centre where a viscosity dependent barrier is reached which does not allow any further increase in speed, so that the vortex core itself rotates like a rigid rod). Through this regular differentiation of speed, very systematically arranged shear flow movements occur. A similar speed distribution is to be found in the movements of our planetary system. This has been considered in more depth qualitatively by Schwenk (1950) and in mathematical detail by Sonder (1991).

The formations of vortex pairs appear to have an organic character. In anatomy and particularly in embryology, very similar forms are described. The similarities between patterns which occur in flow movements and those which are found in embryos involve much more than mere analogy: in both cases similar shape-creating movements are at the root of their development. In early embryonic development, layered cell units which are in surface contact with one another start to grow at different rates. Because of the combination of these two conditions, the layers start to bend round one another, finally turning inside out and rolling up. This is exactly the same formation movement as in shear flow. I therefore consider it reasonable and justifiable to say that such flow movements conform to natural laws of organic formation.

*Instabilities*

Such vortex streets, seen purely in physical terms, occur in the transition between two stable flow types: between laminar flow, where the fluid flows are more or less parallel, and turbulent flow, where everything swirls chaotically; in between are orderly vortex formations which are still laminar. In this transitional phase where the conditions of one flow type are replaced by those of another, the flow types overlap and reciprocally cancel out each other's forces, so that the system becomes unstable and mechanical determination ceases. It is precisely here, where such instabilities occur, that the greatest variety and number of patterns are created in flowing water. Under these conditions, and only then, do we get the so-called 'harmonious flows' (Rapp/Schneider 1974) which, permeated by the natural laws of organic shape formation, reveal themselves as organized phenomena.

All these fluid processes take place in a state of weightless suspense. Because of this, certain external forces, those that normally act upon our earthly condition, are neutralized within the fluid. As the dominant physical forces largely cancel each other out, the inherent instability of the system now becomes receptive to more subtle influences of a kind which cannot assert themselves under more stable conditions. Only now can more gentle forces, those that mainly guide shape formation in organic nature, intervene and determine events.

It is not flow mechanics themselves that determine form in organisms; rather through the presence of instability, flow mechanics open the way for the intervention of organic creative forces within the flow movements. In this respect, Rudolf Steiner described a number of examples of how a higher matter occupies a lesser matter and can be active in it because in the lesser matter the normally dominant forces cancel each other out (for example, Steiner 1922, Steiner/Wegman 1925). The liquid matter does not organize and emerge creatively from its own self. As an open system, it allows itself to be organized through the effects of interrelation with outer events. Water behaves thereby as a liquid continuum, as a whole system.

A further example where the natural laws of organic nature reveal themselves in flow is in the case of a rotating vortex in a closed receptacle. The vortex accelerates towards the centre. Ever increasing in speed and becoming tighter, the vortex rotates down to the depths of the receptacle until blocked by the bottom. Now the vortex must widen and slowly travel back up. Both of these phases are repeated in rhythmic sequence. Directly observing this phenomenon, we find that the unmistakable image of the heart's rhythm of systole and diastole suggests itself (see Fig.5).

What can only be touched on briefly here is treated in greater depth in Theodor Schwenk's book *Sensitive Chaos,* first published in 1962. Exploring water as a mediator of life, Schwenk's work examines the insight that *organic* natural laws are at work in the flow movements of water.

Looking at water, it is decisively important to differentiate between what it represents as a still and shapeless mass and what happens when it moves and flows. When water is in movement, the full abundance of the life-mediating activities of water reveals itself, and movement

Figure 5.    *Left:* the spiral path of a whirlpool; *right:* fibre network of the left chamber of the human heart (from Schwenk 1962).

in turn affects the water itself. It is within movement that those instabilities described above can take place, opening the opportunity for natural laws of organic formation to take effect in the flowing water. As a result, water in flow is able to act as a mediator of life.

*Intelligent order disposition for metamorphosis*

In an experiment designed by Theodor Schwenk (1962), a white-coloured water flows slowly into a clear, still body of water. Resulting from the encounter between the moving water and the still water, suspended in one another, an apparently organic flow form emerges, progressively developing and metamorphosing (see Fig.6).

All here appears in perfect and intelligent relationship. We observe nature at work in creating order, an order emerging and being guided by intelligent activity at some higher level — a process from wisdom through movement to form creation. This is a good example of Goethe's principle of the 'tension of opposites.' In the meeting of two opposites — in our case, between movement and resistance — the result is not a mutual effacing or levelling out but rather a new

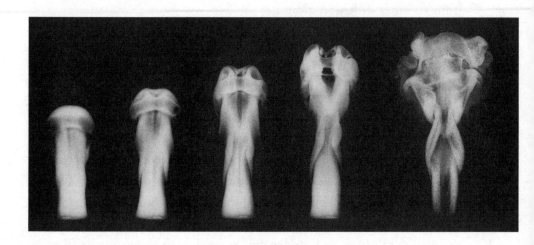

**Figure 6.**    A coloured stream, slowly and steadily flowing into a still body of water (from Schwenk 1962).

development, which emerges through metamorphosis. What we refer to as 'forms' here are only captured and held still as forms in photos and in our minds; in water itself they are but momentary, transitory phases (which essentially have no duration) of a ceaselessly creative process of formation and transformation. In the very moment in which the forms are captured, they are already changing. Their existence is part of their transformation, which lasts as long as movement occurs. As soon as the movement fades, the forms disappear. Only by consciously entering into these transformation processes, can one's mind adequately comprehend water. Water creates patterns and can give us a tremendous abundance again and again, but nothing of this is held fast. Even as it tends towards creating something, it is in the process of dissolving it, creating the opportunity for something new as soon as there is the slightest stimulation of movement. Transformability is the basis for renewal activity. Only in stationary flows, an example of which was mentioned previously, can water retain and hold its shape. This is only the case when water constantly flows through, continuously recreating the form. Once stilled in the same space and place, water is unable to retain any form resulting from an inner differentiation.

## Aspects of time: the natural laws of the cosmos

Everything which takes place in water — building as well as dissolving processes — happens in temporally-structured flow movements, which though operating in space, belong entirely to time. This realm points beyond more than just a spatial and earth connection. The natural laws which prevail in flowing water are not only of an organic nature, as already described, but also of a cosmic nature. Observing the surface of water, one can become aware how it orientates itself in relation to the Earth with its physical surroundings. In the state of buoyancy that we observe accompanying bonding and breaking of bonds, cosmic forces operate from all sides, all of equal importance.

True universality is present within water. The speed profile of a potential-vortex shows close relation to the laws of movement which govern our planetary system. The orientation of small suspended bodies which are introduced into such a vortex also demonstrate the cosmic alignment of water. The speed of the vortices becomes faster towards the middle. Within this motion, as a result of shear movement, a small swimming body is still always orientated in the same direction — much like a eurythmy dancer, who on stage always looks towards the audience, even when she is moving to the side or back. (Only in centrifugal rotating vortices with rigid angular velocity are the suspended bodies orientated towards the centre, like the moon to the earth, always turning the same side to the middle.)

One of the discoverers of the connection between flow movements and the stars was the painter Vincent van Gogh! By expressing his visionary understanding of the night sky run through with flow movements, he was a hundred years ahead of his time![1] Just over one hundred years later in 1992, Steven Shore published his *Introduction to Astrophysical Hydrodynamics*. According to Shore, almost all phenomena known today in astrophysics are most appropriately describable with hydrodynamic mathematical equations. Interestingly, Shore does not speak of 'hydrodynamic astrophysics,' but rather 'astrophysical hydrodynamics,' thus implying that it is the natural laws of the cosmos which manifest in flow movements. In the preface to his book, Shore writes: 'The universe is the most wonderful hydrodynamics laboratory imaginable. Every kind of flow we observe in terrestrial environments occurs in the cosmos on a truly grand scale.'

Because we know that form-creating flows depend on the presence of instabilities, in conditions where the mechanical-physical earth influences are suspended, and that these form creating flows do not arise from the material properties of water alone, why shouldn't we ask ourselves: aren't these cosmic laws revealing themselves in the flow of water? Following through this line of questioning is definitely worthwhile. We are at a point where we can say that not only are the organic laws of nature present in flowing water, but that they are also cosmic laws.

We recall a remark made by Rudolf Steiner where he discusses the four elements and invokes the image of an ancient Greek talking to a contemporary of our times: 'If only you knew what we call "water." Then you too would have an element which as soon as it becomes alive and active is not merely affected by earthly conditions, but is rather the element "water" which in its overall effectiveness is governed by cosmic conditions' (June 24, 1921). In another places, too, for example in his series of lectures on warmth, Steiner describes fluid water as infused by earthly as well as cosmic natural laws (Steiner 1920). But he is most particular at this point with his distinction and precision: 'as soon as it becomes alive and active.' Water is described as infused by cosmic natural law when in an active, not a passive, state. Steiner then adds that the ancient Greeks considered cosmic conditions to be the same as organic-vegetative laws!

How can we characterize the phenomena of earthly and cosmic natural laws and how does water fit in with them? The earth is home to solid substances; they have an external form which is stable and fixed to a certain place. The order of the cosmos, in particular the planetary cosmos, has no bounds towards outer space but inwardly is differentiated, namely as a time-structured creation. The planets circulate around the centre, the outer ones more slowly, the inner ones with a shorter cycle than the earth, so the planetary cosmos is a thoroughly differentiated creation, which draws its order and form out of movement.

Between these is water: in the sphere of a drop it reveals something cosmic. As a liquid substance it has finiteness, and as such is orientated to the Earth, not receding into the air but rather held spatially within certain boundaries. Nevertheless, within these boundaries water shows an unbelievable ability to move and appears in the most differentiated time-structures, which develop and undergo transformations. Another polarity is the permeating and suffusing in dissolving in contrast to the delimitation of the boundary of solid substances. With water a very clear transitional situation can be observed, with elements of the earthly as well as cosmic poles.

Crystals, which appear on earth in close proximity, represent isolation to an extreme of totally lacking connection. The planetary cosmos, in contrast, is an interacting system, which can only exist and be considered as a whole. The planetary system would not be capable of life were it not a whole system coordinated in all its details and subtleties. It is a created order with inner reciprocal influences conveyed in and through movements. Such a reciprocal interaction is found again in the buoyancy of water.

With solid bodies, the orientation follows gravity towards the centre of the earth; in the cosmos, orientation is universal, in all directions. In water, both take effect: flowing downhill, water follows earthly conditions, which gives rise to the creative processes which then take place in time. Dissolved, it obtains in buoyancy an orientation towards its entire circumference.

## The history of human awareness of water

In antiquity, humans experienced water as godlike. Nature and divinity were one. A good example is found in Homer's *Iliad*, which takes place two to three thousand years before our time: Achilles' fight with the river Meandros before the city of Troy. The fight against the raging waters is described as a fierce wrestling match between the hero and the river god himself. Later on, humans perceived the influence of the gods in water and water bodies, but no longer saw them as gods themselves; rivers, lakes, oceans and other water bodies became places of residence and activity of the gods. During this period, considerable awe and respect was shown to water, but physical water was separate from the divine being. Godhead was external to water, although it still exercised influence upon it (for example, Psalms 104).

We can find a number of images of heavenly beings who intervene in water. There are icons which show the water wonders of Chonae.[2] According to legend, the archangel Michael saved a sacred sanctuary in danger from a torrent of water which malicious people wanted to direct into it. Such accounts of the manifestation and influence of heavenly beings in water decrease steadily until water comes to be thought of as no more than the work of the gods. We see here the stages described by Rudolf Steiner (1924/25) as heavenly histories, mythological histories and earth histories.

In the Middle Ages, the same change occurs in the West and continues into modern consciousness. The stages of this change can be clearly followed in art. In the Hita Codex, which dates from the beginning of the eleventh century, a depiction of Christ's Baptism in the river Jordan shows the river not just as stylized water (character-istic of later representations) but as a living whole, teeming with fish and water plants.[3] The river is portrayed as a god and named as *Jordan fluvius*. This kind of interpretation, though, is lost as time passes. Medieval depictions such as the visions of Hildegard von Bingen, show divinity as now external to nature; the divine may encompass nature but nature itself is no longer understood as divinity.[4] In the worldview of Scotus Erigena, divinity is portrayed as standing outside this world: creation, and humans, too, have been separated from the divine world and must return to it. Our earthly domain composed of the four elements (earth, water, air and fire) is seen as a small area surrounded by the planetary spheres, the regions of the zodiac and a hierarchy of angels until one finally arrives at divinity itself.[5] God now lives outside his own creation. In a picture showing God measuring his creation, he is shown stepping into the picture from outer space.[6]

In many pictures from the Middle Ages, one can find representa-tions of water in the sky, beyond the sun and moon.[7] We can con-nect these to an interpretation which goes back to Genesis: on the second day of creation, a separation of the waters took place, so that the sky itself was actually part of the separated waters. The skies and the waters are accordingly of one nature, and of one shared origin. What could be truer than to recognize that the people of earlier times experienced the energies of the skies in water!

From the eleventh to the thirteenth centuries, a spiritual move-ment emerges which ascribes the highest level to the spirits which govern the four elements: in the *Prüfeninger Codex,* for example, one finds the four beasts representing the Cherubim attributed with the names of earth, water, air and fire. Here water is assigned to the bull.[8] In some book illustrations of this time, we see representations of Luke, the evangelist who is inspired from the bull Cherub, shown with water attributes such as water currents or a fish.[9]

There are reliefs from the Romanesque period, too, which show the life-creating flows of paradise — life and flow as one — flowing out of God down to earth, separating and then meeting another corresponding flow from another direction, joining this and together rising up and leading to, depending on their origin, the different life forms (Fig.7).[10] With time, even this interpretation of direct and

Figure 7.   Column capital in the Romanesque parish church in Oberstenfeld, Germany (from Schwenk 1962)

unmistakable provenance from God is lost. Up to the late Middle Ages, people still perceived elementary water beings connected to certain water bodies, such as nymphs and undines.

The beginning of the modern age brings in a new and dramatic change. This is illustrated aptly by the researches of Leonardo da Vinci: humans — until then seen as microcosmos and centre of the world — now see themselves as aware and reflective observers separate from nature.[11] The human being is no longer part of nature, nor nature part of him. Leonardo performs and documents experiments of, for example, the currents in channels where obstacles are placed. This is the start of the times where humans try to find out how God made his works and then try to imitate this. God is recognized as a creator and artist in nature, but humans want to take his place. In the sixteenth and seventeenth centuries this expresses itself in the abstraction and systematization of natural relations, particularly of the four elements. At first these appear as part of the macrocosmos in interrelation with the zodiacal regions. Later, the four elements appear only with the assigned properties according to the Aristotelian system of elements as a structured entirety of four without godhead and without the cosmos.[12]

The change of direction of this development is represented in the frontispiece of Salomon de Caus' book about the cause of the moving forces: he shows that one no longer searches for moving forces in divinity, and that the conviction is there that one can take control of these causes oneself and proceed at one's own discretion.[13] This is to be found not just in words but also in illustrations: people experiment with physical apparatus, such as, amongst other things, fountains and twisted pipes. With the technical capacity which they have won for themselves, they regard themselves as the successor of God the artist and dominator of nature. These insights are initially used for artistic creations — for waterworks, creation of parks, architecture — not like today where they serve mainly economic uses and the convenience of daily life. Technology was then totally in the service of the arts.

Later, more precise descriptions of nature, true to detail, serve to portray spiritual moods: nature's moods are seen as bearers of emotion.[14] This comes to an end around the first third of the nineteenth century. After this, nature is portrayed more objectively.[15] Painters like Claude Monet, who spent his whole life wrestling with the artistic representation of water, sought an exactness until water itself no longer appears in the pictures but rather only all that is in it and on it and mirrored from it.[16] Water recedes in the paintings and gives way to other things, things which appear thanks to water. Those who have the opportunity to deepen their acquaintance with Monet's *Nymphaeas* in the Orangerie in Paris will find that after a quarter of an hour or so, one loses one's orientation, as if underwater. The painter perfectly achieves submerging the viewer in water, although it is not water at all which he has actually painted.

There were also old currents of wisdom which were preserved up to the nineteenth century. A fountain from the second half of the nineteenth century in the Odenwald gives evidence of this: where the water springs from the earth and, opening itself to its surrounding, becomes an element serving life, the fountain base is decorated in relief with plant-like organic forms, representations of a heart and pine cone as life systems.[17] Another fountain shows cosmic symbols, a star and sun wheel, above which an opening plant rosette; however, its pine cone is destroyed and the water pipe is now incoherently laid along the outside: the fountain has become a ruin, a relic of the past.[18]

## *Expanding attentiveness — encountering water anew*

How can we proceed to find, in a manner suitable to our times, a way of encountering the relationship between water and spiritual beings? — with the capabilities which we have today thanks to more exact observation and experimentation with nature. When we look beyond mere external, physical phenomena (as it were encyclopaedically), but rather try to find, in interrelation, the relationships between them, only then do we arrive at the level of processes. 'State' passes into 'process' and one can then ascend from the physical to the etheric. When we become aware of the fine sensibilities which express themselves in colours, tones, forms and movements, then we arrive at the level of the animate; this again can occur consciously. And when we become aware of how intelligently these phenomena are composed and work together, we can begin to experience and recognize the spiritual powers which hold sway in water.

**Notes**

1.  Vincent van Gogh, *The Starry Night,* Museum of Modern Art, New York.
2.  Icons: for example, *The Wonder of Chonae,* sixteenth century Novgorod School, Icon Museum, Recklinghausen, Germany.
3.  *Hita Codex* from Meschede, AD 1020, *Baptism in the Jordan.* Hessische Landes- und Hochschulbibliothek Darmstadt, Germany, Hs. 1640.
4.  See for instance, Hildegard von Bingen *Liber divinorum operum,* folio 6r, AD 1230, cited in   Böhme/Böhme 1996, p.213.
5.  Scotus Erigena, from Roob (1996) p.283.
6.  *Bible Moralisé,* originating from Rheims, thirteenth century. Vienna, Austria, Nat.-Bibl. Cod. 2554, folio 1v.
7.  See footnotes 5 and 6.
8.  *Prüfeninger Codex,* from 1200. Vienna, Austria, Nat.-Bibl Cod.12600, folio 30r.
9.  Luke the Evangelist, *Evangeliar* of Otto III, around AD 1000; Luke the Evangelist, *Uta Evangelistar,* Regensburg, AD 1020, Bayer. Staatsbibliotek München, Germany, Clm 13601, folio 59v; Kreuzigung mit Lukas Symbol, *Bernward-Evangeliar,* AD 1000, Hildesheim, Germany, Dombibliothek; Luke the Evangelist, *Limburger Evangeliar,* eleventh century, Cologne, Germany, Dombibliotek, Cod.218, in Legner (1985), p. 429.
10. For example, the column capital in the parish church in Oberstenfeld near Heilbronn, Germany, in Schwenk (1962), image 88; also the parish church in Ancy-le-Duc, Burgundy, France, column capital 'The Four Flows of Paradise' (own image).

11. For example, especially folio RL 12579r, as well as RL 12579v, 12641v, 12660r+v, 12662, in Pedretti (1983).
12. For example, in Roob (1996) pp.40, 45, 342, 674.
13. In: Böhme & Böhme (1996) p.258.
14. For example J.A. Koch, *The Source of Clitunno,* 1825, Stuttgart, Germany, Staatsgalerie; J.C. Clausen Dahl, *Morning after a Stormy Night,* 1819, Munich, Germany, Neue Pinakotek
15. For example, J.W. Schirmer, *Sea Surge,* 1836, Karlsruhe, Germany, Staatl. Kunsthalle.
16. For example, Claude Monet, *Les Bords de la Seine à Giverny.* Paris, Musée du Louvre. *Nymphaeas,* Paris, Musée de l'Orangerie.
17. Fountain on a farm in Lampenhain, Odenwald, Germany.
18. Fountain on a farm in Eiterbach, Odenwald, Germany.

First published in German as 'Wasser, das universelle Lebenselement.' In: *Elemente der Naturwissenschaft,* Dornach, 74, 2001. Translated by Jessica Read, slightly shortened.

Michael Jacobi

# 4. The Forms of Drop-Generated Images

When I think of the very essence and being of water, the mood of a fresh, cool, bright, sunny morning comes to mind, an experience of clarity, openness and liveliness. What we find in the course of our water observations is at times accompanied by this mood. The movement of water and, above all, the nature of that movement, form and mould those experiences. Even the sight of the play of waves in a river or lake communicates something living and refreshing. Water, in the words of our late friend Professor Ernst-August Müller, is 'movement become substance.' In response to even the tiniest of impulses, water answers with movement. Through its abundance of mobility, water exhibits phenomena which reveal how open and receptive it is to its environment.

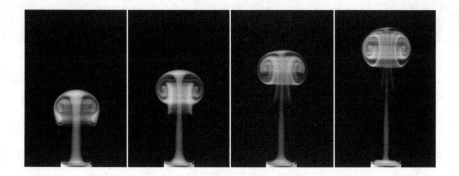

**Figure 1.**  Coloured water is pressed out of a tube and generates a rising ring vortex, seen here from the side. The centre of its inner, rotating movement is shaped like a ring. This ring layer should be visualized perpendicular to the image view here. Four development stages (Photo A. Wilkens)

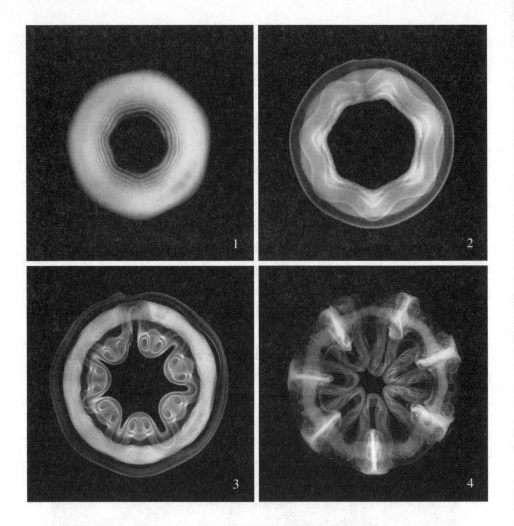

**Figure 2.**   Rising ring vortex, seen from above (from Wilkens *et al.*
1997/2005).

From movement comes form. Thus, through its mobility, water
can produce fleetingly temporary shapes and forms which, in the
very moment of their creation, transform themselves and disappear. One of the most impressive of these forms, and at the same
time one of the most independent from its environment, is the ring
vortex.

Coloured water is expelled from a pipe into still water forming a rising vortex ring which appears, when viewed from the side, like a symmetrically mirrored double spiral, slowly wandering through the liquid. One can imagine that both of the visible rotation centres are connected to one another via an invisible ring-shaped line, which forms the middle of the rotation movement.

Seen from above, the same ring vortex appears to move towards us, as a ring-shaped formation with a multi-layered structure revealed by the colouring. As it continues to rise and approach the water surface, the vortex ring subdivides itself, becomes wavy and goes through an increasingly diverse sequence of shapes and transformations. Despite the high complexity of the flow shapes, these transformations show particularly clearly the ability of the liquid to maintain the context and continuity of its shape. Such flow systems are of exceptional beauty.

The movements within the liquid which continuously impel, transform and then destroy flow shapes, are of a very special type: their moving forms remind us vividly of form structures within life organisms. The distant similarity between flow shapes and organic forms implies a latent correspondence arising from the same natural laws of form creation. This fundamental discovery was made by Theodor Schwenk.

Using the drop picture method developed by Theodor Schwenk, this formative ability of moving water can be scientifically investigated and described. This is achieved through the following process: a glass petri-dish (14 cm internal diameter) with a parallel plane bottom is filled with the liquid to be investigated, to a depth of only 1.1 mm. Drops of distilled water fall into this thin film at 5 second intervals, released by a distributor vessel from a distance of exactly 10 cm above. Flow shapes which occur in the thin layer of liquid, and which would at first not be visible, are made visible by using a schlieren optical apparatus and through the light-breaking effect of added glycerine in the testing sample. Now the flow movements can be observed on a projection screen and photographed. All testing procedures are carried out in a laboratory under strictly standardized conditions, making it possible to compare the drop-generated images of water samples of different origins.

In the resulting drop-generated images, three components can be observed: an inner, 'core' zone, or kernel, with strong, at times chaotic, movement; lying further out, an often rosette-like subdivided vortex zone; and finally, surrounding the vortex rosette, slowly forming straight and bent lineal structures, which because of their branching out are called 'dendrites' (little trees). The vortex zone is

**Figure 3.**   'Polymorphic' development type in a drop picture method test (from Wilkens *et al.* 1995/2005). *From above left to below right:* 5th, 9th, 13th, 17th, 23rd, 30th drop-generated image.

A differentiated image with intermediate vortices, vortices and garlands emerges anew from drop to drop. The vortex development progresses through new maxima and minima and becomes permeated with radial linear structures.

particularly evident, and during the drop picture method testing, this area shows new and sometimes surprising shapes after every new drop released into the sample. The leaf-shaped formations which prevail here, are vortices as already described, only with the difference that they unfold themselves very flatly in the thin layer of sample water, only able to develop by extension.

We can describe the appearance of these vortices using a characteristic language. When only a few drops of distilled water have fallen, the vortex formation is graceful and delicate. As the process continues, stronger and more filled out vortices appear. In the last third of the drop picture method test, the images become wrinkled thanks to the appearance of dendrites. Following from this, descriptive terms from the realm of the living must be sought: 'youthful form,' 'mature form,' 'aged form.' Pure, unadulterated springwaters and drinking waters show a development in the sequence of drop-generated images which similarly mirrors a parallel with the living world. Here, the diverse vortex shapes are richly varied, both spatially (within a single drop-generated image) as well as chronologically (within the sequence of drop-generated images). Characteristically, in such pure waters, there are surprises, and so little predetermination in the arrangement of vortices within an image and even less in the temporal succession of image types. By contrast, in most cases of damaged water, the vortices are repetitive, the image succession monotone, the level of predetermination increases and the developmental aspect disappears. This contrast may remind us of the value of species diversity in the plant and animal kingdoms. A broad species diversity is a valid indicator of the healthiness of a habitat, while the appearance of high numbers of only a few species indicates an unhealthy environment.

Experiences with the drop picture method make it logical to use terms and ways of thinking from the realm of the living in order to understand the context of the phenomena. In other words, the flow developments of the drop-generated images speak to us in a language other than that of purely inanimate objects. Obviously,

**Figure 4.**    'Rhythmic Rosette.' Fourth drop-generated
image of a drop picture method test with
a polymorphic development type (Photo:
Institute of Flow Sciences).

we are involved here with intermediate steps between the inanimate
and a living organism, and are in an area of transition. We have
already taken the first step in this transition from dealing with an
inanimate, physical body towards learning to understand the watery
element. Even when water, as we observe it in the laboratory, is not
a living organism, it nevertheless shows in its flow movement images
of organic character, metamorphosis and development: in a word,
images of liveliness

The distinctive shape-creating ability of the water flowing in
the thin layer can be understood as a new property representing a
distinct aspect of water quality which can be added to those already

known, such as the concentration of contained substances. The 'data' or facts of this new quality property are images of flow shapes. And these images speak to us. If we let them speak to us, if we take them seriously, as up until now only numerical data was taken seriously, then we take a valuable step towards understanding the essence and being of water.

First published in German as 'Wie spricht die Formenwelt der Tropfbildströmungen zu uns?' in F. Metzler (Ed.), *Wasser verstehen — Zeichen setzen.* Herrischried, 2001. Translated by Jessica Read.

ANDREAS WILKENS, MICHAEL JACOBI & WOLFRAM SCHWENK

# 5. The Value of the Drop Picture Method

Since the drop picture method has a very specific role to play amongst many other evaluation methods, we would like to offer a few basic thoughts.

Our relationship to the natural world is largely determined by the direction of questioning and of answers we construct. The most common human attitude arises out of our self-centred desire to control and use nature to our own ends. Such an attitude, which fails to recognize any needs in the world other than our own, has consequences which rebound on us, as can be seen by current global environmental problems. The serving character of water cannot be understood when questions are asked in this spirit. Asking what water really is and how it interacts with others arises from a completely different starting-point. Our very attitude must become selfless! The only realities we can truly understand are those which live in each of us. Therefore the researcher himself must change when trying to understand and associate with water. The drop picture method was developed from anthroposophical ideas and is a step in the above-mentioned way of questioning, a way which we feel is necessary for future development. If one wishes to understand the value of the drop picture method, one has to look for different points of view from those which customarily prevail in conventional research.

Research using the drop picture method may be considered on a hierarchy of levels. On the lowest and simplest level we can distinguish differences between various water samples using drop picture experiments. We can describe the forms they reveal in the drop pictures. We thus can experimentally determine changes that may take place, for example, when water has been treated (assuming, of course, that the method is sensitive to these changes). This holds for both material, as well as for dynamic, changes (for instance, by shaking). Here, we have in mind the example of the potentization of homeopathic medicines. The drop picture method is very sensitive to changes in organic substances, in particular, to surfactants (surface active agents). Mineral substances are more closely related to water and only become manifest in higher concentrations in drop pictures. If we are interested in the change in water without going into qualitative aspects, we use this method as indicator in the conventional manner, with the exceptional feature, however, that we are not involved with numerical values but rather with pictures. Thus, rather than being a purely analytic method, it is a diagnostic method.

At a higher level, we use the method effectively as an organ for observing the mobility of water as it manifests itself through drop pictures, for instance, in the course of a river, in technical processes, and so on. Here the region from which the water sample originates and the picture of the water in the experiment mutually illuminate each other. One learns something about the stream, about the water and about the method. Such experiences allow the method to tell its own story and we learn to see how qualitative aspects in the immediate life-relationships where the water originated, begin to speak their own language. We thus gain insight, not only into the qualities of the mobility of water which express themselves in the drop pictures, but also to the way in which these qualities are embedded in their natural surroundings. If this quality is lost by man-made pollution, for example, then a part of the natural life accompanying this water is also lost and, if any, only lower forms of life establish themselves.

We thus acquire criteria for forming assessments and discover a hitherto unknown quality which now gains significance: the mobility of water. A particular value of the drop picture method at this level is that we are able to characterize a good quality drinking water positively by its mobility. A method of evaluation has been developed which allows a critical judgment of this aspect of mobility via the morphology of the vortex forms.

If we imagine two drop pictures, each showing the same number of vortex forms in the above sense, they may nonetheless have a different character and make very different impressions on the observer. One might appear ordered, harmonious and forceful, whereas the other appears chaotic, disharmonious and insipid. In order to capture this sort of aspect, we need a level which gives access to the image aspect of the pictures, a step to finding formative processes active in nature. We find a starting point in this direction in the spa water investigations. Here we find an image of the physiological function which the water addresses as a healing quality. Such examples are only pilot experiments pointing along the path we are seeking.

The significance of this sort of work was described in the following manner by A. Selawry commenting on Ehrenfried Pfeiffer's method of sensitive crystallization:

> This method opens a possibility of bringing the essentials of form to our consciousness today. If we can grasp the activity of a formative world in phenomena, then science will find a bridge from forms to those form-giving ideas or archetypal images. This will open the way to the science of tomorrow. (Selawry, p.90)

First published in Wilkens, Andreas, *et al.*, *Understanding Water*, Floris Books, Edinburgh 2005.

ANDREAS WILKENS

# 6. Flow Movements During Drop Picture Testing

Since the development of the drop picture method by Theodor Schwenk in the 1960s, the Institute of Flow Sciences in Herrischried has researched and described specific aspects of water quality in varied contexts and permutations using this method (Schwenk 2001). We have kept up a constant work of trying to account for the flow processes which occur in the shallow water layer and which produce the diverse and varied flow images (D. Rapp, P. Schneider, J. Schnorr, J. Smith, A. Wilkens). Thanks to experimental work in the last few years, substantial new findings have been made. We are now able to offer a more exact account of the drop-generated image flow process.

New understanding of the flow processes has also made it possible to identify and understand transitions between very different forms in the drop-generated images. In addition, we have observed parallels between the drop-generated images and the characteristics of flow processes.

## The drop-generated image

The drop-generated image is a photograph showing a central excerpt (5 centimetres in diameter) of the flow events occurring within a thin layer of a water-glycerine mixture. The dark line running from the middle to the side of the image is the shadow of the syringe needle used to deliver the drops. The shapes and lines occur due to flow movements between the distilled drop water and the water sample (which is mixed with glycerine). They are made visible using a schlieren optical apparatus. Figure 1 is taken approximately 1.8 seconds after the impact of the twentieth drop.

Three zones with different flow processes and shapes are distinctly identifiable in the drop-generated image. The area in the middle, where the drops fall and impact the sample is called the *core zone,* or *kernel.* In the first third of the testing sequence, the core zone is clearly delimited and internally chaotically structured. Surrounding the core zone is an area called the *vortex zone.* In this area, new vortices are formed following each drop impact. Bordering the vortex zone is an area where, starting from approximately the tenth drop, lineal structures slowly start to occur, growing from inside towards the outside. The lineal structures ramify, gradually filling the whole area. This area is called the *dendrite zone.*

The light-dark quality of the drop-generated images is dependent on the schlieren optical apparatus settings which can be modified or reversed as required.

## *The drop impact conditions*

The flow processes occur in a 1.1 mm thin layer of water. The water is held in a Duran glass petri-dish (inner diameter 14 cm), with a precision polished parallel base and positioned exactly level. The drops of water are released at exactly five second intervals from a syringe needle ten centimetres above the centre of the petri-dish. When the drop of distilled water is released from the needle, it starts to oscillate strongly, completing approximately five full oscillations before it impacts the water sample. The oscillation frequency is determined by the size of the drop and, in this case, by always having the same water composition. During the drop picture method testing procedure, the underside of the impact drop should neither be too convex nor too flat. Consequently, the ratio between drop size (approximately 3 mm diameter) and drop distance needs to be set precisely. Incorrect settings result in completely different flow shapes and insensitive testing conditions (Wilkens/ Jacobi/Schwenk 1995, 2000).

**Figures 1–3.**

1. Drop-generated image after twenty drops of good, clean water. Polymorphic and developed vortex unfurling can be observed;
2. A drop-generated image with a medium grade vortex unfurling (at drop number 20);
3. 'Garlanded' drop-generated image at drop number 17, without vortex unfurling.

## Chemical and physical relationships
## between impact drop and water sample

Due to the impact of the drop of distilled water, primary flow occurrences take place in the test sample. Secondary flow occurrences can take place when there is a reaction between the impact drop and the water sample. If these two are chemically and physically similar, they are mixed together only very slowly by diffusion. This does not affect the primary flow occurrences. Where chemical and physical strengths are balanced, subtle differences between the drop and test sample can become apparent through the unstable phases of flow movements during the development of the image — these tests are very sensitive. In a case where the drop reacts with the water sample, strong secondary flow occurrences prevent orderly flow occurrences and forms from taking place. These tests prove to be insensitive and unrevealing (Figure 5. See for example Smith 1975, Wilkens/Jacobi/Schwenk 2000).

## The addition of glycerine

The addition of 13% weight glycerine to the water sample serves to make the flow processes more visible and is chemically relatively inert in relationship to the water and its contained substances. There is no chemical reaction, but physical parameters are changed, whereby the relationship between drop and sample has a specific tendency: the water sample becomes more viscous, which slightly slows down the flow occurrences; the flow occurrences become somewhat more dense so that compact layering occurs; the surface tension is somewhat reduced, resulting in a compensation movement in the sample surface from the periphery towards the centre; there are also concentration differences which slowly adjust through diffusion — as a consequence the schlieren flow shapes are slower

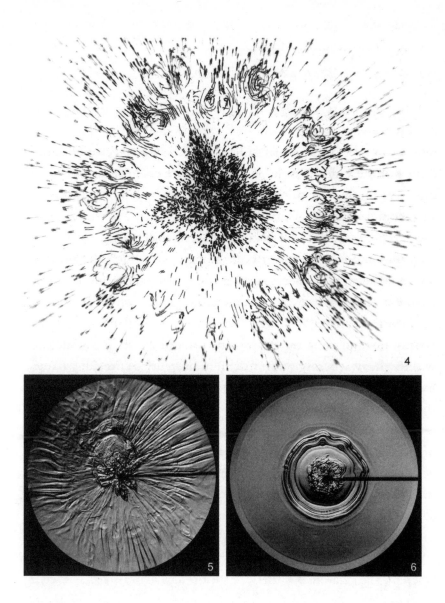

**Figures 4–6.**

4. A drop-generated image with plant pollen spores and without glycerine, shown with lateral lighting on a dark background and long exposure time (negative print);

5. A drop-generated image of a sample with 5% ethanol (after 27 drops);

6. A drop-generated image with a tenside dilution 1/50000, after 20 drops.

to disappear. Thus, glycerine is an important modifying factor in the development of the flow shapes.


## The impact process of the drop of distilled water

The impact of the drop of distilled water on the thin water sample layer forms a crater which can extend to the bottom of the petri-dish and pushes the water into a ringed wave. From this wave, a succession of capillary waves emerge (see Fig.10). A return move-ment rapidly follows the initial abrupt displacement, so that the crater is closed again within milliseconds. When a drop falls from a greater height into deeper water there is no such ring of waves. Rather a segmented crown occurs with splashes which are thrown up into the surrounding area (see Fig.7). A similar segmentation process takes place in the drop picture method test, only concealed within the wave ring, not reaching the surface (see Fig.8) but inclined towards the vortex zone (see Fig.15). After the closing of the crater, the fluid of the distilled water droplet is almost all in the centre of the impact area (Figs.11–13). The next drop pushes the liquid of the previous droplet out of the core impact zone into the vortex zone. The vortices are observable using schlieren optics or ink colouring (Fig.14).


Figures 7–14.
  7. After impact of a drop of ink in deep water;
  8. As 7 but in shallow water;
  9. Plant spores on the surface of the drop spread out on the surface of the sample after drop impact;
  10. Sample surface after impact of the drop of distilled water, drop picture method testing conditions;

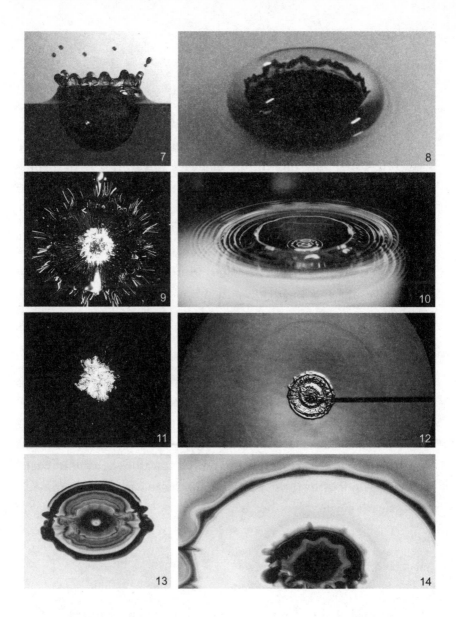

11. Plant spores within the droplet remain in the impact zone of the sample after drop impact;
12. A drop-generated image after the first drop impact;
13. The ink from a drop of ink has almost all returned to the core impact zone;
14. A second drop has pushed the ink from the preceding drop into the vortex zone.

## Vortex formation

The vortices in the vortex zone occur in the first milliseconds after the impact of the drop of distilled water. Using schlieren optics they initially remain concealed (Fig.10) under the first succession of waves. Using ink and diffuse lighting (Figs.14, 15) or plant spores and lateral lighting on a dark background (Figs.16–18) it is possible to make this first flow movement visible. A ring vortex occurs (Fig.14) which draws water out of the core impact zone, sweeping pollen spores from the bottom of the petri-dish with it (Fig.16). The vortex axis has a rotation direction, the water flows from above out and then down to the petri-dish centre (Figs.17, 18). Segmentation then sets in, and local thickening occurs from which the so-called drop-generated vortices emerge (Fig.15). The formation of the drop-generated vortices may stop at an embryonic stage, or continue through all its phases until it reaches full development (Figs.1–3). The return flow mentioned above distorts the first occurrence of the vortices. There are two types of vortices which can then form, usually alternately with one another. Short, wide intermediary vortices mostly located towards the core impact zone (Fig.1, one above, three below), alternate with long stemmed vortices with small vortex heads.

**Figures 15–23.**
  15. Individual vortices develop out from the garland ring vortex;
  16. The garland ring vortex sweeps spores with it from the bottom of the petri-dish;
  17–18. Traces of the displacement of spores in a narrow light beam, starting at their brighter part; 1/300 second light exposure on the plant spores; section through the vortex ring at arrow;
  19–20. The spread ink forms a pattern as it sinks;

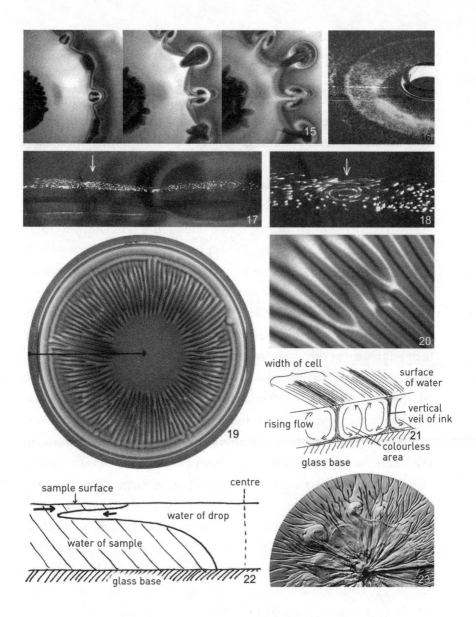

21. Section through the flow rotation during the sinking of the ink;
22. Section through the water sample during testing;
23. Detail of a drop-generated image (fortieth droplet) with strong dendrite formation.

## Vortex formation without glycerine

Tests carried out using plant spores and long exposure with lateral lighting on a dark background show that similar drop-generated flow processes occur without glycerine. In Figure 4, the alternating arrangement of the short intermediary vortices towards the middle and the long stemmed vortices towards the outside is clearly visible.

## Vortex development as an assessment tool

Observation reveals that in comparison to good quality spring water, the degree of unfurling and development of the vortices decreases as the water quality declines. This can also be shown in testing series using increasing dilutions of organic, surface tension active sub-stances (Wilkens/Jacobi/Schwenk 1995, 2000). The resulting forms all represent transitional development stages of a vortex somewhere between its initial unfurling and full development. A purely morpho-logical inspection of these forms allows a corresponding ranking of the forms, based on the degree of vortex development. Thus a system of reference numbers based on vortex development stages has been established. This is particularly useful in bigger testing series, where sometimes only minimal differences are observable, and a compara-tive ranking order is an important analysis tool. Generally, samples of good clean water have a high level of vortex development (Fig.1). Samples of contaminated water on average show limited to no vortex development in the drop picture method testing (Figs.2, 3 and 6).

## Surface and volume — different classes of phenomena

The surface of the drop of impact water behaves differently from its volume. On impact, it does not disperse into the water sample but

**Figures 24–29.**

24. Standard testing with distilled water *(aqua distillata)* and increased laboratory temperatures (25°C, droplet no.25);
25. Same as 24 but with lowered laboratory temperatures (15°C, droplet no.25);

All the following images occur after the twentieth droplet:

26. 3% saline solution;
27. 0.25% acetic acid solution;
28. North Sea water from 15 m depth;
29. Water from the river Rhine, near Basel 1972.

actually spreads itself on the surface of the sample (Fig.9). After the first drop in the testing sequence, the very delicate disc of the spread droplet surface is visible (Fig.12). In contrast, the fluid volume of the drop totally submerges in the sample, as one can see when plant spores are used (Fig.11).

Because of the difference in surface tension between the impact droplet and the glycerine-mixed water sample, a compensation reaction happens on the surface of the water sample: when the impact droplet has a higher surface tension than the sample, which is generally the case, the surface in the core impact zone contracts, the surrounding area being pulled as a consequence. This develops into surface movement from the periphery towards the centre, which draws with it some of the water immediately underneath. This in turn triggers a return flow movement deeper down.

When surface tension active substances (tenside, for example) are present they build a mono-layer on the surface and make it more viscous. This can effectively immobilize the surface and hamper flow movements beneath it, to such an extent that no vortices or dendrites occur (Fig.6).

## Layering

A compensation movement in the sample surface due to differences in surface tension can lead to unstable layering in the sample. Sample water is layered over the impacted and spreading drop water (Fig.22). As the water sample is mixed with glycerine it is denser, making the top layer unstable. The sinking of this top layer gives rise to a distinctive pattern that we call 'dendrites' (Fig.23).

## Lineal structures in the dendrite zone

Tests with spreading ink have helped understand the development of lineal structures. Blue writing ink released from a syringe needle on to the water surface spreads out and forms a thin layer. Because the ink is denser than the sample, the layering at the water surface becomes unstable and the top layer begins to sink in various places. This sinking occurs into a water layer which has systematic flow behaviour: on the surface the ink flows or rather spreads from the centre towards the outside, in volume a reactive movement takes place towards the centre. This movement propels the sunken ink into radial arranged lineal structures (Figs.19, 20). The ink sinks as a thin vertical veil (dark line), spreading out on the bottom of the petri-dish (lighter area). In the area adjacent to where the ink sinks, another return movement takes place, the surrounding water moving up (colourless area). Pairs of these rotating cylinders occur, their diameter depending on the depth of the sample. They create relatively constant distances between the line areas, where the ink has sunk (Fig.21).

The unstable layering described above in the drop picture testing leads to similar lineal structures as in the spreading ink tests. The denser sample water sinks into the impacted drop water creating similar lineal structures, often in a radial arrangement. Differing here from the ink test behaviour, the layer of water above flows towards the drop impact centre and below it moves away (Figs.22, 23).

When there is equal surface tension between the sample and the distilled water of the impact drop, there is no spreading tendency, no unstable layering and no lineal structure formation. Some lineal structures do occur because of density differences between remains of vortices. But these lineal structures are different, being mainly curved and concentrically arranged (Figs.24, 26).

Test samples with a viscous surface mono-layer and without vortex formation generally show no lineal structure formation (Fig.6).

## Testing the developing process

A drop picture method test is usually carried out to forty drops. During the test, distilled water from the drops accumulates to some extent in the core zone which can lead to layering. Each new drop falls into the fading flow shape of the previous drop, and thus slightly different conditions. Within the context of the whole test, the initially clear, sensitive shapes become ever more complex and reciprocally overlapping. At the beginning, the core zone is clearly defined (Fig.12). With increasing drops, its boundary softens (Fig.1). The vortex zone is renewed with every drop but with increasing drops becomes less clear and more bisected with lines (Fig.23). The dendrite zone develops slowly in parallel with the slow formation of layering. By the end of the test, the entire dendrite zone is filled with lines (Fig.23).

The vortex unfurling in the drop-generated images of relatively clean water can vary from image to image. An image with no vortices can alternate with one with many vortices and vice versa, with every possible intermediate variation. A test can start with the appearance of many vortices and end with few or none. This development process of the vortices can be characterized with the help of a numeric vortex unfurling ranking system (see p.78). This allows a comparative characterization of the sample to be graphically portrayed (Wilkens/ Schwenk/Jacobi 2000).

## Time aspects of the drop-generated image zones

The core zone, or kernel, is the area where the drop of distilled water impacts the water sample. In this non-homogeneous and in part chaotic area of flow shape, each successive drop encounters slightly different conditions in the core zone, which influence the subsequent flow patterns. So seen, it is as if the core zone contains an incipient outline of the flow movements to come, predisposing the character of the subsequent segmentation of the drop-generated image. The core zone has a relationship to the future.

The vortex zone is renewed with every drop and is relatively independent of the arrangement of vortices of the previous drop-generated image, and similarly of which drop number the testing is at. The vortex zone belongs totally to the present.

The dendrite zone is a significantly more lasting occurrence, which starts slowly, growing with every drop, ramifying and eventually filling the image. The arrangement of lineal structures reveals something about the history of the test. If the test had for example few vortices, the lineal structures are evenly spread in a radial arrangement. If there were for example lots of large vortices, the radial arrangement is overlayered with dynamic curvatures. The dendrite zone at the end of the test has undergone a development. It has a relationship to the past.

## Polarities

### A geometric polarity

Wrapped, curved shapes and directed, straight shapes are the main elements of the forms in drop-generated images. The vortex head lines and concentric curved lines point to one pole, while the radial arranged dendrite lines point to the other. Both form groups occur almost always together, but it can happen that either one or the other is more or less developed or dominant (Figs.24–29).

### Polar flow movements — polar shape gestures

A simple experiment can show that specific shapes occur because of specific flow movements. When a liquid flows out of a reduced opening (a pipe) into an open basin, it spreads, slowing down, and when the liquids are for example different colours, an identifiable front formation is visible. The incursive liquid bends convexly, and inside-out shapes occur, such as spheres, mushrooms and vortex heads. In this spreading flow movement, a round spot of ink would be shaped to a quarter moon, concentrically orientated towards the flow source, in this case the mouth of the pipe (Fig.30).

In the case of the opposite flow, where the fluid accelerates from the surroundings towards the tight opening of the pipe mouth, all areas of the liquid show a directional orientation towards the pipe opening. In this case, a round spot of ink is drawn by the closing and accelerating flow into a long shape, which points towards the pipe mouth (Fig.30). Thus:

❖ spreading flow movements result in rounded concentric shapes;

❖ closing flow movements result in radial shape arrangements (Wilkens 2002).

*Polar flow and shape creation in the drop picture testing method*

As the drop of falling distilled water impacts the water sample, it pushes the water out to the sides. This spreading, slowing movement creates rounded, convex shapes (including for example, the wave ring). As part of this, a vortex ring develops, which subdivides into individual vortex elements. The head of each of these

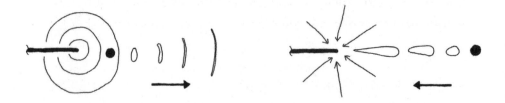

**Figure 30.** Schematic representation of shaping of a spot of ink. *Left:* in a spreading flow movement; *right:* a closing flow movement.

vortex elements shows the flow gesture of the spreading, slowing flow movement. They are rounded and convex. All these flow movements are instigated by the impulse of the plunging drop of distilled water.

Two return movements follow on from this first impulse: firstly, the central crater closes and the chaotic core zone is established. Most likely, surface tension plays an important role here because the crater closes very quickly. Depending on the sample, a second return movement also occurs, from the periphery towards the centre. This movement occurs on the surface and is instigated by spreading tendencies between the drop-water and the sample. It is a closing movement which results in layering and lineal structures. This second return movement has a very different character from the first. It has nothing to do with the physical impulse of the drop, but with interactions of substance properties (surface tension, density) between the drop-water and the sample. The resulting flow movements are, in polar contrast to the concentric rounded ones, orientated radial lineal structures (Wilkens 2001, 2002).

## Polar drop-generated images

Drop-generated images with mostly rounded, concentric, curved shapes (Figs.24, 26, 28) and drop-generated images with predominantly radial, lineal structures, unmistakably give an impression of extreme opposites. Experimental tests as described above help explain how these specific shape characters relate to a specific flow movement. In an extreme case of rounded, curved, concentric shapes, there is little to no contraction of the surface towards the centre. The flow movement gesture of spreading is dominant; the spreading 'front' of the drop water is undisturbed (Figs.26 & 28). The water from the drop remains on the surface. No unstable layering occurs, and subsequently no radial lineal structures.

In the opposite extreme case, a strong contraction of the surface towards the centre occurs (see above). The spread fluid of the drop is covered with sample water (Fig.22). Shear flow takes place between the unstable layers. The denser sample water sinks into the less dense drop water, resulting in lineal patterns. This contracting movement of the surface is form-creating and regulating, an impression which is clearly readable in the drop-generated image (Fig.27).

Figures 24 and 25 show no such strong extremes. Clean water samples from, for example, good springwater tend to be more balanced and do not show such extremes. Unstable layering occurs, but does not dominate. It gets mixed up by ever recurring vortices. As such, the shaping principles of spreading and contraction are held in balance, each given expression (Wilkens 2001, 2002).


## Parameter testing

The drop picture method testing is always carried out under standardized conditions. This is to allow optimal expression and observation of the actual sample properties (Wilkens *et al.* 2000). By changing test parameters, drop-generated images can be obtained which relate to different water samples. Thus parameter testing can contribute to the characterization and understanding of different waters. This principle can be illustrated by looking at three parameters:

### Sample quantity
When twice the amount of sample is used compared to the standard amount (20 ml), the vortex development is lost in the volume of the sample, spreading little to the sides, and uncontoured, rounded shapes dominate. When half the amount of sample is used the vortices do not unfurl. Shear flow between the surface and volume and the contraction of the surface dominate, and radial lineal structures occur. The diffusion in uncontoured forms of a bigger volume and the cramping of the shallower volume can be clearly observed in the images.

*Viscosity*

The addition of less glycerine leads to loose, contrast-poor and diffused forms. Rounded shapes predominate. Increased glycerine content results in a tighter and smaller image, interspersed with sharply contoured, close, radial lineal structures. This 'freeing' and 'inhibitive' effect is evident and observable in the drop-generated images.

*Temperature*

For this comparison, the whole laboratory is warmed up to 25°C or cooled down to 15°C. The petri-dish, distilled water and water sample are all at laboratory temperature. At the warmer temperature, the drop-generated image is larger (Fig.24). The unfurling of the vortices increases, the vortices themselves are bigger. Lively, curved forms and many rounded lines occur. The image gives the impression of wide, open, rhythmic curving impulses. Tests carried out under the cooler conditions are quite different (Fig.25). The image is smaller and looks contracted. The vortices are small; radial lineal structures dominate. In this comparison, the elementary impression of warm and cold are evident: extension and contraction, flexibility and rigidity can clearly be experienced.

## Dilution testing

Practically no test parameter can be changed without having ramifications on other parameters. For example, when the test temperature is changed, the density, viscosity and surface tension of the water sample also change. This is also the case when substances are added to the water sample, for example salt or acetic acid. Particularly in the latter, significant surface tension effects of the sample become prominent. Concentrations are chosen so that a 3% saline solution increases surface tension by 0.5 millinewtons/meter (mN/m) and a 0.25% acetic acid solution decreases surface tension by 0.5mN/m.

In the saline solution test, the surface tension difference between the drop-water and the water sample with glycerine is approximately equalized; with the acetic acid it is doubled. As explained in the previous trials, the effect can clearly be understood. The saline solution (Fig.26) shows only rounded, curved forms, as there is no contraction of the surface. The acetic acid trial shows a strong surface contraction with the subsequent layering and occurrence of radial lineal structures.

The development of shapes is completely related to the water flow development. Yet it is a surprising discovery to see how the impression of the shapes communicates something of the character of something salty and something acidic. Salt has a dissolving, soaking and swelling aspect. Brine is a lubricant between the fingers. Acid contracts, slows, makes two fingers stick instead of slipping against each other. These same impressions are given by the drop-generated images.

## Water samples from nature

By varying the test conditions and water samples with known parameters and substances, much can be learned about the 'language' of drop-generated images and about water and its interactions with different conditions. When water samples are taken from nature, their composition and properties are normally not known. In these cases, it is essential to already be conversant in the 'language' of the drop-generated images. Most revealing is when the exact context of the sample is known, so that the drop-generated images and natural properties and context of the sample can inform about one another. A highly illustrative example is the investigation of a section of self-purifying river in the Black Forest (see p.113). There the drop-generated images were compared with chemical and biological analysis and fauna counts taken at the same sample points (Peter 1994).

Two other examples from nature show the polarity that we have discussed here. A saltwater sample (Fig.28) taken from the North Sea at a depth of 15 metres (where water is cleaner than on the surface) shows a distinctively 'salty' drop-generated image. A fresh water sample (Fig.29) taken from the Rhine near Basel in 1972 clearly shows pollution, which had reduced the surface tension. It is a typical expression of the river at that time, a body of water which assimilated and picked up many things along its way. Happily, today the river Rhine is much cleaner than in the 1970s.

## *The drop picture method is process specific*

The investigations discussed above showed a certain polarity arising under completely different conditions. This makes it clear that the function of the drop picture method is not to identify properties of the sample or aspects of the testing conditions based on signatory shapes in the drop-generated images. To this end, physics and chemistry can be used. Rather, it is an image representation of a process which occurs in the water during testing, revealing fields of action of a more universal nature, for instance, closing or unfolding. Working with the drop picture method can help identify the character of a good quality water, suitable for higher life, meaning specifically drinking water, holding these polarities in balanced unity.

First published in German as 'Strömungsvorgänge beim Tropfbildversuch und Beziehungen zwischen Probe, Strömungsprozess und Bild,' in: *Elemente der Naturwissenschaft,* Dornach, 81, 2004. Translated by Jessica Read.

CHRISTINE SUTTER-PICARIELLO

# 7. Evaluation of Drop-Generated Images

The drop picture method allows water the opportunity to express itself freely. The resulting images are like a language that we try to read and understand during the testing and from the photographic documentation. Learning to 'read' the images is a never-ending process. It is a skill that develops with the observer's experience, awareness and consciousness. The following account describes the stages of evaluation of drop-generated test images in my work.

## Preparation

First, the entire series of test images is checked through for aberrations to see if the experiment has been carried out properly. Tests with abnormalities clearly related to working conditions (which in fact rarely occurs) are rejected. Two to three films from the control tests are selected as neutral samples. As the general development character of the drop-generated images can be different from series to series, the control samples are used to provide a reference for each test series. The remaining tests are then anonymously coded, an essential step to ensure the impartiality of the analysis.

## Observation

One by one, starting with the control sample, the test images are examined with calm focus. This is a moment of perception, of inner, peaceful receptiveness and warm attentiveness. Free from preconceptions, the mind of the observer is allowed to be infused and imprinted by the movements which are the source of the images. This activity is similar to a breathing process. Not only the optical senses receive impressions. Mostly unconsciously, touch, balance and movement senses are also stimulated via the optical senses and contribute to the impression.

After observing a test film of twelve drop-generated images, a general impression is imprinted in the mind of the observer, leaving an inner picture. This inner picture becomes clearer the more often it is recalled to the mind of the observer.

As a simple exercise, let's look at three drop-generated images: A, B and C.

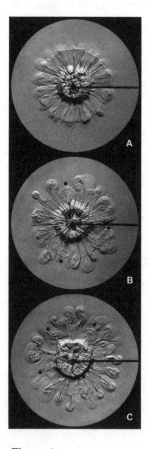

### Description

Here the task is to appropriately describe and communicate the wordless impressions captured by the drop-generated images.

The summary inner picture is a general but characteristic impression of the entire test series, as if one had fluently conversed in the 'language' of the phenomenon. To translate the observed 'language' of movement into words is however frustrating and often inadequate, as words are limiting and full of associations. In order to help characterize these flow processes which have been reduced to fixed images, a range of descriptive terms can be used:

Figure 1.

❖ The movement process: for example image A, 'contracted-rigid,' image B, 'balanced unfurling,' image C, 'dancing swirl';

❖ The sensual-mood impression: image A, 'stifled,' image B 'quiet, slightly reserved,' image C 'gay and serene';

❖ The atmosphere of the flow movement as eurythmic colour atmospheres: image A 'dark blue, almost grey,' image B, 'blue-green,' image C, 'yellow';

❖ The morphological image characterization according to the unfurling of the vortices based on Jahnke (1993): image A, 'garland,' image B, 'garlanded-rosette' and image C 'rosette.' In cases where special gestures and forms, such as the bowl-shaped vortex groups in picture C, help characterize a test, they are additionally noted.

## *Evaluation*

Once the nature of the individual test images has been summarized in words, it is important to compare and contrast the various test samples. Differences are often already spotted during the observation phase. At this point, they are now compared with the reference control sample. It is important to identify which distinguishing features best describe the differences in water flow within the context of this particular test series.

For qualitative evaluation, depending on the nature of the images, the following can be used as additional indicators:

❖ the type of border edging of the core area, expressed as core types (Wilkens *et al.* 2000);

❖ the degree of vortex unfurling, expressed as vortex types (Wilkens *et al.* 2000): type 2 for image A, type 6 for image B and type 8 to 9 for image C;

❖ ranking of the tests based on a particular characteristic (such as more or less 'dancing' vortex wreaths as in image C).

Some differences can also be quantitatively assessed, such as:

❖ the frequency of particular vortex types (possibly expressed as vortex type number);

❖ the number of a particular form characteristic, such as the bowl-shaped vortex groups in image C;

❖ the number of intermediary vortices such as short, wide without a stem. Image A has none, images B and C, 3 each (see black dots in Fig.1);

❖ at what point during a test, specifically at which drop number, does the vortex wreath start to be radiated through with dendrons?

Quantitative analysis of distinguishing features helps evaluate and generally qualify the processes in drop-generated images. They are provable and countable. The numbers can be formulated algebraically and statistically analysed. With a small, limited test series, qualitative assessment methods are usually enough. However, quantitative evaluation makes sense and is a useful complement when, for example, results need to be presented to an unpractised public, or for large test series with many similar images, where the perceived differences need to be portrayed based on specific characteristics. Quantitative evaluation is also useful for planetary constellation test series, where samples of the same water are tested over a long period of time. Here, likewise, standardized criteria are needed to compare series over an extended period of time.

This whole evaluation path takes the 'reader' from the initial perception of an inner picture, to describing the movement processes, then to the selection of criteria and parameters and statistical analysis should this appear necessary. He or she is aware that this path leads away from the original, pure perception: criteria and parameters are only an impression of the actual phenomena. If I were to begin the evaluation based on predetermined criteria, I would immediately bar the possibility of learning the true 'language' of the images. This language gradually starts to reveal itself when space and place is allowed for receptive attentiveness, and when I consciously take the time and effort to repeatedly recall to mind the perceived inner picture. When one feels one has got a grasp of the language and through this a feel for the water movement, it still remains tricky to translate and convey this information while staying true to the original.

## Decoding

Last of all, the films are decoded revealing which sample belongs to which test series, or for example which samples show accordance with astronomic occurrences. Making connections between the test results, the type of sample and the astronomic constellation when the tests took place is a thrilling moment — often one is simply left standing in amazement!

First published in German as 'Schritte der Auswertung von Tropfbildern,' in: *Elemente der Naturwissenschaft*, Dornach, 81, 2004. Translated by Jessica Read.

WOLFRAM SCHWENK

# 8. Formative Processes as an Aspect of Water Quality

Our aim is to describe an aspect of water quality which can be discovered and called forth from within the water itself. Our search should not be motivated solely by wanting to avoid negative assessments (that is, defining quality by the absence of certain elements) but should positively reflect some characteristics of water's own nature which can be understood as a picture or sign of its life-mediating activity. Therefore, the research procedure itself should invite water to express its nature and in so doing, reveal its own inner characteristics.

Could we, then, find in water — the mediator of life — some characteristic aspects of life itself and could we discover how these relate to the very character of the water ?

## Life

Physical matter in its dead state is either unformed or else takes a form governed by the laws of its own substance. In contrast, material in a living state takes the form of the organism and so is governed by a higher principle from which it takes its direction. Here, the various substances of the organism do not dominate but act in a serving role.

For this change to take place from one state to the other, the material has to be freed up within a watery fluid medium. In this way, water serves as a mediator of a higher ordering principle, and the higher principle needs to be active within the water itself.

Life exists as a continuous process; it goes through development, it does not come to rest in a completely stable state. Even when life processes exist in a flow equilibrium, they fluctuate rhythmically, adjusting bit by bit in relationship to each other. A prerequisite for this is inner mobility in the organism.

Organisms (in general) live in continuous interaction with their surroundings: their openness is essential.

## Water

For water as a life-mediating element, the same qualities are characteristic. They manifest especially through its streaming movement: 'Water responds to the tiniest of impulses with movement. To the extent that one can say: water is substance become movement.' (E.A. Müller, Foreword in Wilkens *et al.* 2000). Water movement expresses itself as streaming. We find within water those formative processes which fleetingly appear through a continuous coming and going of fluctuating boundaries between differentiated volumes. The inner mobility of water makes this possible: here, forming and development are the same; they are inseparable. The formative processes in moving water take place in a 'system' in connection with a higher principle through which specific details are integrated and ordered, the same as with an organism.

The activity of forming takes place as long as movement is stimulated in the water. If this happens continuously, it arrives at a flow equilibrium of constant (stable) streaming; if discontinuity happens, new forms are created through continuous transformation. They are brought about and changed until they fade away with the end of movement. Once in a state of stillness, the water cannot hold on to the fleeting forms. They appear in water together only when there is movement. This dynamic does not occur at all without movement. After the movement has stopped one can find its traces at best with the help of other materials also carried along with the streaming.

The fundamental characteristic of water is its openness towards peripheral influences — it is given over to these peripheral forces — and in a certain way it is defenceless. Given this vulnerability, it has to absorb and accept pollution of all sorts without having the chance to choose.

The variety of streaming forms develops depending upon outer conditions. Through observing this, one can come to see the extreme dependency of water behaviour upon outward conditions. Water can only be understood in context with its surroundings and not isolated from them. Taking into account this openness of the water to its surroundings is essential for understanding how water appears and the importance of its function.

We thus find a susceptibility of streaming water towards forces from outside as well as from within the water itself, modified by materials with which it has been in contact and which it has dissolved and absorbed.

The inclusion of water in life processes has its dynamic on the boundaries between water and living organisms, with their organs or parts of organs. If one understands the general principles of water behaviour already, as an expression of its affinity with life processes, the behaviour of its movements in boundary layers will be understood and described even more clearly.

The drop picture method serves as an instrument to show the differentiated way of these qualities in water and as attributes of life with the help of the behaviour of movement through thin layers. We have published accounts of the method along with many of the results (see references below) so here I will give only some basic ideas.

The drop picture method does not force particular movements upon water. The opportunity for water to move is given through the drop picture method under standardized conditions. In this way the actuated movement can allow water to express itself with its own characteristic behaviour and qualities.

In the multi-formed drop picture, streaming conditions exist in balanced relationships. With this pattern the water is provided with the greatest possibility of openness. Where we have weaker and less multi-formed streaming patterns and less mobility, the images show that the forces influencing the water monopolize its openness and do not let it show its full capacities. Such forces are able to work from the outside physically, for instance, through electrostatic fields. But mostly they arise from the influence of diluted substances which modify the physical characteristics of the dilution through such parameters as surface tension, density and viscosity, so altering those mutual relationships which influence the streaming. It is these mutual relationships, and not only the size of one or the other, that are decisive. Through such influences (e.g. diluted substances) the diversity of streaming may be limited in favour of specific streaming types.

Diluted mineral substances influence the relationships only in higher concentrations, for example through high mineral content of mineral water and through sea-water, but not in ordinary concentrations in drinking water and natural fresh water. But organic substances often shift this relationship immediately with very fine dilutions, thus influencing the behaviour of movement even at low concentrations. However, the streaming pictures of the drop picture method allow no conclusions as to which actual substances participate in this shift: they do not show what water contains but rather, how it behaves in its movement itself.

The qualities of naturally pure, unpolluted groundwater give water specialists a benchmark for good drinking water. The drop picture method takes these reference points for evaluating the positive qualities of good drinking waters. Such natural groundwaters are already by their nature hygienically flawless, refreshing and enlivening, and they give the impression of liveliness. They have energy and variety in the forming of drop picture streamings. This behaviour can be understood as an image of their active role in organisms.

We must differentiate from this the adjustment of the laboratory standard where steam-distilled water is used as a reference control. Distilled water also moves in a multi-formed manner but is less intensive and less diversified in its forms than fresh, pure spring groundwater. Using this standard one establishes a middle value. Only when you have a sufficiently median balance point do you set up the conditions for the widest openness in *all* quality directions. Then the method is given sufficient sensitivity, and, by virtue of the instabilities in the streaming, allow formative forces coming from the periphery to operate in a shape-forming manner in the water. Polymorphic drop-images and drop picture experiments reflect these procedures.

The intensely formative quality of water that we see in multi-formed drop picture streaming, is found in nature where generative activity dominates the metabolism within the water. The renewing capability of such waters is visible in the drop picture streamings in the traces of form-building processes.

The organic, chemically dissolved substances serve in natural waters as substrata for micro-organisms and set up decomposing processes. Where there is an excess of such material in the water, one observes undifferentiated ring and disc forms of drop picture stream-ings, which repeat throughout the drop picture experiment almost without development. Here we see in the physical body of water the predominance of the microbial digestive process of decomposition and disintegration, rather than generative activity.

In this way, the typical signature of streaming patterns and life processes becomes clear.

The quality of purity, as well as keeping the water clean, is there-fore an essential condition for generative activity within a body of water, and more widely, where water is actively assisting genera-tion. In this view, purity has a positive meaning and significance. Seeing this as a condition for the survival of life, we look beyond the simple prevention and removal of undesirable and threatening substances, in the sense of damage prevention, which is a double negative.

All those who understand water as an element for life and, for this reason, attach great importance to it, will find their most important allies in the ranks of drinking-water specialists and engineers, who struggle to minimize water pollution and so work for the purity of water.

We must be grateful for their never-ending, courageous effort.

In view of the mission of water as a life element and, therefore, the qualities needed for this task, it is justified, to my thinking, to speak of the creative mobility of water as an independent quality-aspect, understanding it as a complement to the hygienic-analytic parameters and other quality criteria. In this way we grasp a positive significance of the importance of the purity of water and therefore add to the searching for understanding the positive character of water as an element for life. Thus we can arrive, too, at an even higher esteem for the uniqueness of naturally pure water.

First published in German as 'Strömende Gestaltung im Wasser als Qualitätsaspekt,' in F. Metzler (Ed.): *Wasser verstehen — Zeichen setzen,* Herrischried, 2001. Translated by Jennifer Greene.

Wolfram Schwenk

# 9. Aspects of Drinking Water Quality

The characteristics that distinguish water as a means for maintaining life become effective when water is in motion. Hence water's mobility as a liquid is its most important property.

In his *Textbook of Food Chemistry,* Schormüller emphasizes that foodstuffs, beyond their chemical and energy-giving characteristics, are organically structured compounds. To this we can add: Water as the most important foodstuff for all organisms is not yet organized, but rather capable and suitable of being organized when moving. By its mobility it has the potential to be reorganized within itself. For this reason one should consider water's mobility carefully as an important aspect of water quality.

If you incorporate mobility into your qualitative analysis of a given sample of water, then you will expand your efforts beyond avoiding disadvantage towards the positive aspect of water's ability to give way to creating and organizing processes. By examining the way that water behaves in flow, you may get a picture of its organizational potential. Theodor Schwenk's drop picture method is a technique specifically developed to provide a scientifically reliable procedure (Wilkens *et al.* 2000) that can reveal this hitherto disregarded positive aspect.

Using the drop picture method the following results can be stated in general: Naturally pure, uncontaminated well- or spring-water — in other words, ideal potable water that is refreshing — shows in its drop pictures a characteristic complexity of multi-formed flow behaviours. In their flow movements arise a multiplicity of rhythmic form patterns which change with each freshly stimulated movement and which form anew. The mobility of such

**Figure 1.** Examples of drop pictures at the twentieth drop. *Left:* naturally clean springwater; *centre:* processed tap water; *right:* water contaminated with very slight traces of a detergent.

water is at the maximum of its formative capacity. The diversity and multiplicity of flow patterns in such drop pictures is comparable to the ecological strength, in its importance for biology, found in biodiversity. This mobility is not usually attained with hygienically treated drinking water from polluted primary sources. Damaged water flows unrhythmically, is poor in flow patterns and shows less differentiation (Figure 1).

These differences present the possibility for characterizing good water in a positive way. In this light, the protection of natural and pure groundwaters is of particular concern. The organizing activity of water movement establishes an additional category of water quality in its own right as a positive expression of the organizational potential of good, refreshing water. It may supplement the normal and necessary analytical approach to water quality but is neither intended nor suitable to replace it. The study of water motion shows how a volume of water behaves together with all the substances it contains, and also how the latter combine to have a modifying effect on the water's mobility, resulting in particular flow patterns. But such study cannot identify these substances; they must always be tested by chemical and bacteriological analyses.

A water source is potable when it is free of anything that could potentially become a health hazard. In many countries, laws regulate and describe the limits for communal drinking water sources and suppliers. Beyond potability, drinking water is deemed 'good' in a very general sense when it is not only hygienically unobjectionable but beyond that exhibits all the other characteristics of a naturally pure refreshing water. Water's mobility, allowing polymorphic shape creation to occur as described above, belongs to this group of properties. One can sense this 'lively' quality as a refreshing character, which can be experienced with many hard waters too.

Natural purity of water does not only mean a lack of undesirable components, signifying that it is harmless and potable. Moreover, it is the very condition for water's rejuvenating activity by movement and thus for its enlivening function. In other words: purity has a positive meaning; it is a quality in its own right. These observations increasingly challenge us to respect and protect the purity of water. The most important unwritten law in ancient times was to show reverence to all waters and not to pollute them. People experienced the presence of gods at work in these places, a picture worth conjuring up in our minds, since acts of creativity continue to take place even today in clean moving water if we allow them.

## Tips for handling drinking water

Because of the special sensitivity of pure water, many of our human habits actually affect the natural freshness of our drinking water. A great number of the problems that lead toward dissatisfaction with our drinking water supplies are of our own doing. By handling the drinking water supplied to us properly, we can usually preserve its characteristic goodness. Problems in this regard occur, for example, when water is allowed to stand for hours and days in pipes under

**Figure 2.**    Drop pictures. *Left:* from city tapwater after many hours of
stagnation in the pipes; *right:* from the same tap after running the
water to flush the pipes.

pressure and increased temperature (Fig.2). Add to this the possibility that the pipes are made of synthetic materials, or the fact that the
water may be stored in plastic containers.

The best method for ensuring that your drinking water is fresh,
therefore, is to allow it to run sufficiently before you use it for drinking or in the preparation of food. This means flushing all the residual
standing water out of the pipes and letting it run until its temperature is evenly cool. But try, however, not to waste the water that is
being flushed out, rather try to collect it in a pail or large container
and use it where the freshness is secondary, for instance, in house-
cleaning tasks or flushing the toilet, and so on.

Proper planning when building or renovating a house should pay
attention to the fact that those rooms needing access to water should
be placed close together, thus allowing pipes to be as short in length
as possible and with short branches only.

Nowadays, plastic materials are used in the storage and transport
of drinking water and are preferred for many reasons; among others

**Figure 3.**   Drop pictures. *Left:* from drinking water after being in a pipe
made of PP-R (polypropylene-random copolymer) for twenty
hours at 20°C; *right:* from drinking water after being in a high-
grade steel pipe (V4A) for twenty hours at 20°C.

they are cheap, lightweight, easily moldable, non-corrosive, and insu-
lating. But most of such materials commercially available at a reasonable price tend to leave traces of chemical compounds in the water
which is in contact with them. All these by-products of plastics are
foreign to the water and do not belong there. They inhibit the sensitive mobility of water. It is best to avoid using such products when
installing water pipes in a building or when storing water for personal
consumption. The best choices for such purposes involve materials
such as glass, porcelain, hard-glazed pottery, stoneware or enamel for
storage, and stainless steel for pipes (Fig.3).

To preserve the best qualities of fresh water, pure glass bottles or
containers are more favourable than plastic ones (Fig.4). Most mineral waters sold in bottles are not a reasonable alternative to drinking
tap water that has been officially proved to be unobjectionable, for
most types of bottles affect water quality adversely due to either their
material or their history (insufficiently rinsed) and due to the material of their screw caps.

**Figure 4.**    Drop pictures. *Left:* from distilled water from a synthetic bottle; *right:* from distilled water from a clean glass bottle.

In general, when deciding which materials should be used for water conduit piping, the crucial factor is the chemical character of the local source of water. In the case of waters that are corrosive by nature or when waters of different origins are supplied alternately, it is important not to use copper pipes as conduits. The latter are then in danger of corroding and releasing dissolved copper in the water. This can lead to insidious copper poisoning, particularly for young children. With adults, the effects of subliminal copper poisoning appear at first in the form of chronic indisposition and nausea. Wherever copper pipes are used as a conduit for tapwater, it is particularly important to flush them out regularly and thoroughly before using any of the water for preparing food or drinking.

Lead should not be allowed to come into contact with drinking water. It is poisonous and easily dissolves in water. If you have still lead water pipes in your old house, its surface may be protected by the fur of hard water. To avoid lead poisoning, this water must not be softened by using domestic water-softeners in your home.

In addition, here are a few comments regarding various methods that have become fashionable for treating and handling the drinking water in our homes:

Normally, follow-up treatment to water that comes from local public sources is not required if you handle the water properly. The water coming from calcium-rich sources demonstrates as much lively mobility as that coming from primary rocks. You can get this impression from observing such sources in nature as well as from drop picture flows. In fact, the drop picture method shows no correlation between the level of freshness of a water and its calcium content. The dissatisfaction that people experience with 'hard' calcium-rich waters arises from other undesirable qualities such as the crusty calcareous deposits in pipes and containers due to temperature increase and the coagulation of organic compounds by forming muddy films and coatings. But in this process of forming compounds, the calcium not only removes aromatic substances from food and drink, it also inactivates undesirable compounds that may be dissolved in the water. These activities are inhibited when you apply a water-softening device, thus causing unwelcome effects. Generally speaking, a lack of freshness of drinking water will not be restored by water-softening technologies.

If you still find it necessary to install a water-softening unit to avoid build-up of deposits in your plumbing, then you may divert one pipe of untreated cold water to the kitchen in order to have access to unaltered drinking water close to where food is prepared.

Any of the various domestic technologies that retreat and reprocess drinking water must be serviced regularly and carefully, otherwise they become a health hazard. This is true not only of ion-exchangers and filters of all different kinds that demand regularly to be flushed, or in some cases, regenerated or replaced.

If you decide to purchase a calcium-converting device using magnets, you should consider the fact that the extremely fine particles of suspended calcium crystals tend to form muddy deposits in the expanded areas of pipes, such as boilers and pressure-equalization tanks. In such cases it is advisable to provide appropriate devices for emptying these areas, even if the supplier of the units claim that they need no servicing.

Ion-exchangers which use rock-salt to substitute the calcium content of the water for sodium ions, can pose a danger to those individuals who need to follow a low-sodium diet. Masking the calcium in water by adding phosphates is not recommended from either a nutritional or an ecological standpoint.

Reverse osmosis is a process that presses water through semi-permeable membranes, whereby it separates out the compounds that are dissolved in water. These compounds are held back by an ultra-fine sieve. In order to flush them away, usually twice as much water is needed as that which is purified. In efficient units it is possible to achieve almost chemically pure water. But usually the equipment necessary for such water purity is not supplied with units installed in homes. The water from these units will then eagerly dissolve all soluble substances with which it comes into contact, for instance, plastic softeners and heavy metals in the tubes and containers, without bringing along with it the minerals that would bind such substances into compounds and thereby inactivate them. Thus, such treated waters can become more unfavourable than the untreated ones. Long-time use of drinking water that has undergone reverse osmosis is only advisable with certain prescriptive diets. Otherwise it is as unreasonable as a diet based only on products derived from fine wheat flower. In general terms, the same measures as described above concerning domestic water treatment apply to reverse osmosis as well.

Many people will experience the switch from existing tapwater to a water which has been modified by any one of the methods just mentioned as refreshing and even enhancing their wellbeing. But this usually subsides after they have become accustomed to it, and then may even turn to the contrary. Any changeover from one type or brand of water to another will affect and mostly stimulate one's metabolism; whether this changeover is from a mineral-deficient to a mineral-rich one or vice versa does not seem to matter. A proper judgment regarding which type of water is more wholesome can only be arrived at when the long-term effects of the water have been determined. This normally depends on the individual, and a general statement or recommendation is not possible.

If you enjoy bottled mineral waters as a refreshment, you should change your brands from time to time. Most mineral waters act as natural medicines, and as with medicines, you should not get used to them. Choose whichever brands give you a good flavour as well as a feeling of wellbeing. But don't replace all your drinking water with bottled water.

The experimental results illustrated above for different waters were obtained by the Institute of Flow Sciences by applying the drop picture method. Such indications about quality of drinking water can only be used in general terms for bringing about an understanding in these matters. The Institute does not possess the means to undertake the specific analysis of certain products, and for this reason cannot give any information or recommendations regarding the appropriateness of certain water-treatment methods or any brand-name products involving water quality. The principal mission of the Institute of Flow Sciences is to extend understanding of the nature of water, a resource so vital to the support of all life on our planet, by developing a thinking that is adequate to the fluid character of water.

Modified extract from Wolfram Schwenk, *Das Wasser als lebenvermittelndes Element*, Ulm 1995.

WOLFRAM SCHWENK & CHRISTINE SUTTER-PICARIELLO

# 10. Study of a Section of a Self-Purifying River

The evaluation of water quality in lotic (flowing water) systems relies in principle on the analysis of physical, chemical and biological characteristics. Our proposition here is to study a new descriptor of water quality, not just based on its constituent elements but taking into account the most outstanding characteristic of water as a liquid: its ability to move and flow, an essential function in its role as a life mediator. The hydrodynamics of water can be shown by using the drop picture method. We looked at this new criterion of hydrodynamic behaviour and applied this methodology along a length of stream polluted at point source by biodegradable organic effluent, and compared the results with customary testing parameters.

## Study framework

Between 1972 and 1977, ten testing surveys were carried out on the Mettma, a mountain stream in the Black Forest, in collaboration with the Institute of Limnology, University of Freiburg (Germany). The Mettma is a trout-inhabited stream, oligotrophic and with a low flow rate (150 to 1500l/s). At a certain point, a brewery discharges organic pollution into the stream, in quantity equivalent to the raw effluent of six thousand inhabitants. Subsequently, the stream crosses a wooded mountainous zone and has no other interference apart from a dilution factor of 3 due to small tributaries. The duration of the study was terminated by the installation of a treatment plant at the brewery in 1977, and was spatially limited by the construction of a weir nine kilometres downstream from the effluent outfall. The study includes 11 sampling stations, one upstream and further stations respectively 50, 300, 700, 1450, 1800, 3000, 3900, 5100, 7150 and 8000 metres downstream of the effluent outfall. In this article, we use results collected in testing surveys carried out during periods of low water (192 litres/second).

## Analysis and sequence of physical-chemical parameters

### 1. Temperature

The introduction of effluent and the resulting additional bacterial activity increase the stream temperature from 10° to 13°C. The temperature reduces only slightly over the total study section of 8000 metres.

### 2. pH

The Mettma is naturally slightly acid, with pH values typically between 6.1 and 7.0. Immediately downstream of the effluent outfall, pH values oscillate between 6.1 and 10.4 because of the neutralization of the effluent. The pH levels stabilize after 3000 metres.

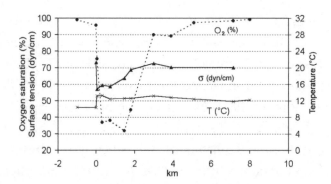

**Figure 1.**  Evolution of temperature, dissolved oxygen and surface tension along the length of study section of the self-purification stream (Peter 1994).

## 3. Surface tension

The initial surface tension values correspond to water free of surface-active substances, but decrease drastically at the effluent outfall from 73 to 57 dyn/cm. The brewery effluent is chiefly composed of organic matter. At 3000 metres downstream, surface tension values stabilize at levels somewhat inferior to initial values.

## 4. Dissolved oxygen

Close to total saturation upstream of the outfall, the dissolved oxygen values drop dramatically to 35% at the outfall due to the high oxygen demand of bacterial activity and oxidation of organic matter. Oxygen levels progressively return to their initial values 7150 metres downstream.

## 5. Ammonium and phosphates

Ammonium and phosphate ions are introduced by the effluent. Phosphates reach maximum concentrations 50 metres and ammonium 300 metres downstream, products of the breakdown of the introduced organic matter. These pollutants are totally metabolized at the downstream checkpoint of 7150 metres.

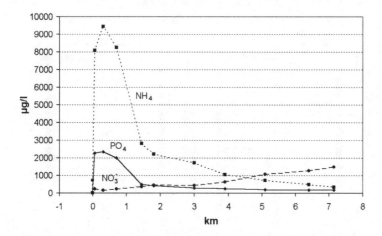

**Figure 2.**   Ammonium ($NH_4$), nitrate ($NO_3$) and phosphate ($PO_4$) concentration in µg/l.

### 6. Nitrates

A product of the oxidation of ammonium, nitrates are initially only present at low levels. Their concentration increases progressively along the length of the study section, levels not having totally stabilized at 8000 metres downstream of the effluent outfall.

## Biological analysis

### 1. Evolution of the biotic community

Initially, the Mettma is a balanced stream ecosystem, oligosaprobic (very slightly polluted in the saprobity system of evaluation) and typical of the trout zone. It is inhabited by a wide variety of animal and plant species that constitute its biotic community. Forty different species of benthic fauna are indicative of this diversity.

The brewery effluent adds an organic charge comparable to the raw effluent of six thousand inhabitants. This profoundly modifies the ecological equilibrium of the ecosystem. The system becomes polysaprobic (heavily polluted according to the saprobity system). Life conditions favour the development of filamentous bacteria *(Sphaerotilus natans)*

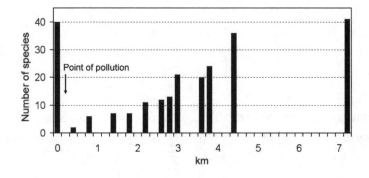

**Figure 3.**   Number of species (taxa) of animals on the stone substrate during the course of the self-purifying section (after Schreiber 1975)

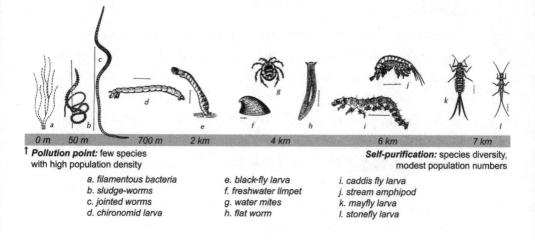

| | |
|---|---|
| **Pollution point:** few species with high population density | **Self-purification:** species diversity, modest population numbers |

| | | |
|---|---|---|
| a. filamentous bacteria | e. black-fly larva | i. caddis fly larva |
| b. sludge-worms | f. freshwater limpet | j. stream amphipod |
| c. jointed worms | g. water mites | k. mayfly larva |
| d. chironomid larva | h. flat worm | l. stonefly larva |

**Figure 4.** Typical representatives of the benthic fauna the length of the self-purifying stream section (according to Peter 1994).

and ciliates and exclude other species. In this first, polysaprobic zone which stretches for approximately 300 metres, the number of benthic species plummets to two. The filamentous bacteria eventually detach themselves and are transported several hundred metres further where they deposit and become important nutrients for colonies of sludge-worms *(Tubifex tubifex)* and chironomid larvae *(Prodiamesa olivacea)*. This degradation zone, where the breakdown of organic matter dominates, ends with the appearance of black-fly larvae *(Odagmia ornata)* and monocellular algae 2000 metres downstream of the outfall point. This marks the beginning of the primary production zone, with a succession of vegetation species from algae and mosses to superior vegetation. Species of herbivores, such as freshwater limpets *(Ancylus fluviatilis)* and mayfly larvae *(Baethis rhodani)* as well as carnivores such as stream amphipods *(Gammarus fossarum)* and predatory larvae of various insect species reinhabit the biotope. The trout zone is fully regenerated after about 7000 to 8000 metres, the number of fauna species in the benthic zone reattaining its initial value.

*2. Polarities*

If we take into consideration the evolution, distribution, variety, morphology, mode of nutrition and locomotion of the benthic fauna, the following can be observed:

❖ At the beginning of the self-purifying study section, species diversity is very reduced while population density is high. The organisms generally have a homogenously segmented morphology with radial symmetry. Sensorial organs are very primitive. Most organisms are sedentary and saprophagous (feeding on dead or dying animal matter). Their rhythm of activity depends only on the supply of nutrients, their life activity being orientated towards metabolism.

❖ At the end of the self-purifying study section (as upstream of the effluent outfall) there is greater species diversity, while the population numbers remain modest. The morphology of the organisms is more complex with heterogeneous segmentation, axial symmetry and a greater body surface area. Sense organs are located at the head, organisms are more mobile and are herbivores or carnivores. They follow day-and-night and seasonal rhythms. Their activities are orientated towards sensory functions and locomotion.

## Hydrodynamic analysis

### The drop picture method

The drop picture method allows the study of water's aptitude for movement, its hydrodynamics. The method involves the systematic and controlled agitation of a shallow water sample through drops of distilled water released at five second intervals. The impact of each drop of distilled water on the water sample creates internal movement and flow forms. The addition of a miniscule amount

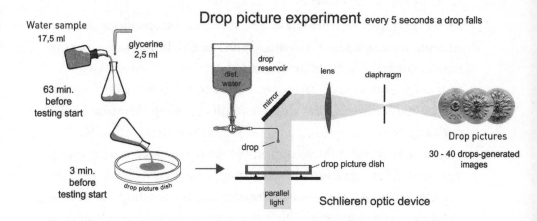

**Figure 5.**   Drop picture method procedure.

of glycerine to the water samples enhances the visibility of the flow movements in a schlieren optical apparatus so that they can be photographed. Successive drops renew the created flow movements, so that a whole series of thirty drop-generated images can be recorded.

The drop picture method was examined in the 1990s to optimize and standardize the testing methodology. Results are usually interpreted qualitatively, but may additionally be analysed based on quantitative analysis of for example the degree of development of vortex forms. The drop picture method indicates the given movement capacity of a water sample based on the level of complexity and differentiation of its internal flow forms. It is a morphological method, complementary to physical-chemical analysis, revealing information about the hydrodynamic qualities of a water sample, but not its chemical composition. It is a system to evaluate water based on positive, life-giving criteria, rather than the exclusion of negative criteria.

*Application to the section of self-purifying stream*

The testing points are identical to those of the previous studies. The water samples are analysed on the same day as they are collected. Thirty images are produced for each water sample. Here the twentieth is selected to facilitate comparison between samples. We will now discuss the most distinctive phases along the stream self-purifying section.

Upstream of the effluent outfall, the drop-generated images reveal a garlanded rosette of vortices where more extended vortices alternate with more stocky ones. Leafed vortices can be observed, as well as radial dendrite structures. The image is relatively balanced, showing

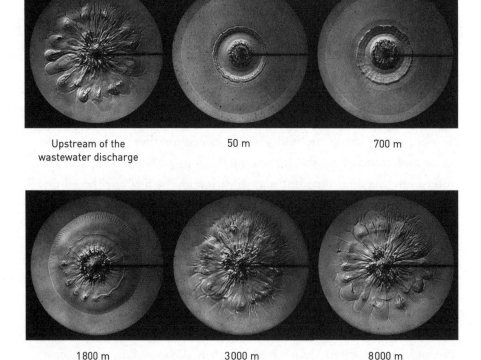

Upstream of the wastewater discharge                50 m                700 m

1800 m                3000 m                8000 m

**Figure 6.**   Drop-generated images after the twentieth drop along the section of self-purification.

differentiated and varied structures which are freely renewed with each successive drop.

Downstream of the effluent outfall, the drop-generated images are totally different. They are simply and solely composed of a disc-shape structure centred on the central point of impact. The forms are rudimentary, undifferentiated and monotonous.

1800 metres downstream, the disc-shape structure shrinks while in the centre the beginnings of differentiation, the buds of heads of vortices can be identified.

About 3000 metres downstream, the beginnings of leafed vortices and dendrites can be observed again. The closed disc-shape form has disappeared.

By the end of the studied stretch of stream, the internal flows return to moving variedly and complexly and are as differentiated and polymorphic as upstream from the effluent outfall.

## Comparison of the different descriptors

### Physical-chemical parameters and hydrodynamic evaluation

The evaluation of the hydrodynamics of a given water sample is not based on any one drop-generated image but rather on the evolution of the ensemble of images. At some point each of the samples reaches a point of inflexion, where after a certain number of drops the garlanded rosette shrinks, disappears and is replaced by a more rigid radial structure. This is what we call the 'point of inflexion,' which occurs sooner or later in the tests, depending on the hydrodynamic qualities of the sample in question. This is a useful parameter. The drop number at which it occurs can be used to compare water samples taken along the length of study stream in question. When a disc-shaped structure appears in the first drop-generated image, the point of inflexion has already taken place before the start of the testing.

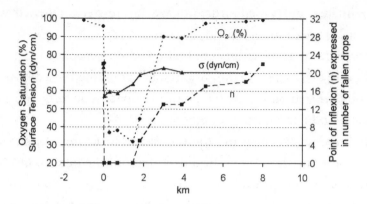

**Figure 7.** Evolution of oxygen saturation, surface tension and point of inflexion (Peter 1994).

The graphical comparison of the levels of oxygen, the point of inflexion and surface tension demonstrate a connection between levels of oxygen and the point of inflexion. This relationship is however not causal but demonstrates that there is a correlation between these two factors and water quality. In most of the measurement surveys, the evolution of physical and chemical parameters stabilizes well upstream compared to where the point of inflexion stabilizes. This in contrast only returns to its pre-effluent levels at the very end of the length of studied stream, parallel to the re-establishment of the biotic community to its initial levels. The point of inflexion appears to be a sensitive descriptor, indicative of the overall state of the stream ecosystem.

## The biotic gradient and stream hydrodynamics

It appears that along the stream in question, after the effluent outfall, there is the least species diversity, and the presence of sedentary, simple-structured organisms, whose activities are confined to their metabolic activity. This is where:

(a)  the drop-generated image, in reference to previous images, has a closed and monotonous disc-shape;

(b)  the drop-generated image shows a lack of mobility and a pre-determined evolution.

In addition, we note that upstream of the effluent outfall and at the end of the stretch of self-purification, where biotic populations are varied and balanced, individual organisms have a more differentiated anatomy, complex nutrition and locomotion as well as being more sensitive to their environment due to more advanced sensorial organs — this is where:

(c)  the drop-generated images reveal a maximum of polymorphic, diverse flow shapes, with the greatest complexity of movement in the water, and where the images have a differentiated structure without being predetermined in their evolution.

## Conclusions

This comparative study of the physical-chemical, biological, and hydrodynamic characteristics of a self-purifying section of the Mettma proves that there are parallels between the degree of diversity in the biotic community and the degree of movement diversity in water samples from the same testing stations. In the degradation zone, where metabolism processes determine the physiology and activity of the animal population, water samples show monotonous and weakly defined flow shapes. In the primary production zone, where thanks to primary production by vegetation, anabolic processes dominate, the water samples show in contrast diverse and differentiated water flow shapes. Thus, very different phenomena can carry the same signature of a shared intrinsic quality. Physical-chemical parameters are descriptors of a specific moment of the stream. The biological indicators reveal a more integrated long-term picture of the water, whereas the hydrodynamic analysis reveals the momentary but holistic state of the water.

First published in French as 'Suivi du parcours d'autoépuration d'un ruisseau par la dynamique de ses eaux.' In: *L'eau et le monde vivant,* Congrès de la Société Hydrotechnique de France, Paris, October 2004. Translated by Jessica Read.

WOLFRAM SCHWENK

# 11. The Role of Substances in Formative Processes

We encounter living and non-living substances in nature in a huge variety of shapes and forms. The forms of the mineral world are dominated by angles and edges, smooth faces and fractures. In living bodies, we observe how formative gestures — rounded and pointed, swelling and invaginating, encapsulating and spreading, fusing in intertwined planes — combine to create form. How significant are the substances contained within them for the creation of these forms?

In the world of minerals, the shape of a crystal is determined by the substance of which it is made. Sodium chloride forms cubic crystals, quartz hexagonal, and calcite rhombohedral ones, while citric acid appears as rhombic prisms, and benzoic acid as flakes, and so on, with impurities creating variants. In non-living nature there is a tendency for forms to be substance-specific and incoherent. Laws 'inherent' to the substances govern here (Steiner 1904/1922). Today this style of observation — expressed as precise descriptions of pure solid substances — has been generalized into an all-inclusive and universal scientific worldview. Specific conditions, such as heat, pressure, disturbance, motion, concentration, and impurities, can influence and modify the origination of the resulting form. These factors may determine what type of crystal will arise — for example, whether calcium carbonate crystallizes as calcite or aragonite. However, the conditions do not in themselves produce the forms. If the formation of distinct crystal structures is prevented in a mixture of substances (granite, for example), rudimentary forms or amorphous agglomerations will appear, rather than clear structures of a distinct type. Here the conditions of origination arrange the various forms to create an impression of individual elements coexisting, but almost unrelated, in a haphazard and completely or largely uncoordinated configuration.

Only in exceptional cases does one mineral adopt the crystalline form of another, that is, when one grows into the pre-existing form of a different mineral by a process of gradual transformation (pseudomorphosis). Here one substance bows to the alien formative principle of another.

Where the substances of non-living nature are in an unsaturated state, they are integrated into the forms of other substances or appear amorphous and formless. Living nature is different. The substances in the tissues and cells of organisms appear neither as formless accumulations nor as random distributions, and only in exceptional cases in crystalline form. The substances become part of an organic form that is determined by the organism itself, and not by what it contains; the substances can do no more than modify the form. Thus the substances become involved in the creation of forms that are foreign to their own typology, and in organic nature this is the rule rather than the exception.

In the organism, substances take their place within a dissolved liquid state from which they are secreted, deposited into their form, filling out its shape. A wealth of different substances is *ordered* sensibly together, in close functional relationships, and then exchanged constantly at close to dynamic equilibrium. The order takes precedence over the individual component, which becomes interchangeable.

The organism integrates the substances into its formative activities, using them, putting them to work. The laws inherent to the substances, which are form-determining in the mineral world, retreat to such an extent in the organism that the substances submit to the *organism's* forms: a principle of shaping *superior* to the substances seizes them and organizes them.

In other words, in the mineral world the constitutive laws of physical nature *rule;* in the organic world they *serve* (Schwenk 2001).

This even applies where organisms secrete mineral substances in saturated concentrations. For example a snail's shell or a seashell, which are made of pure calcium carbonate, represent organic forms. They do not take the form of calcite or aragonite crystals, even when the substance is crystalline. Crystalline calcium phosphate enamel is part of the typical tooth form and does not take the pattern of apatite crystals. The skeletons of diatoms and siliceous sponges are composed of pure silica but take on organic forms instead of individual quartz crystals.

So if we wish to learn about the significance of substances in the context of life on the organic level, we have to look at the formative laws of the organism that absorbs and organizes the substances, rather than those of the substances themselves. Rudolf Steiner pointed out that in life the substance is ruled by forces acting from the outside to the inside; the substance 'must obey the forces radiating from the periphery upon it,' while in lifeless nature the determining forces radiate from the substance itself (Steiner and Wegman 1925, chapter 3).

If life leaves the organism — if its formative powers recede — its form disintegrates and the substances that were within it are left once again to the rule of their inherent laws. Friedrich Schiller applied the same principle to human society: 'Society set free, instead of hastening upward into organic life, collapses into its elements' (Schiller 1795).

Of the many different stages that nature realizes as transitions in the polarity outlined here, one in particular is of decisive significance: transition through the liquid state. In the liquid state — melting and solution — non-living substances lose the specific form that they attain in the solid state. They approach shapelessness and become unstable: internally amorphous, outwardly deliquescent, covering and filling up the constraining medium, the surface spreading out horizontally. Their appearance is now merely *state-specific, uniform* among all types of substance.

However, if a force or forces act upon them, they react with internal movement and differentiation, the latter arising through the movement and ceasing when it stops. Differentiation appears in formative processes that are not substance-specific, but common to all liquids. As in pseudomorphosis, the substance obeys an alien formative principle. However, in the liquid this is no longer the formative principle of another substance, but an overarching one that applies to all substances: the formative processes that appear in the liquid as the order of motion are those of organic nature (Steiner 1921, Schwenk 1962, Schwenk 1998/2001).

What an organism organizes for itself and maintains, by its own life, as it develops happens passively in a lifeless liquid, due to agitation within a transitory formative process. In that sense, moving liquid and its inner formative processes are 'at the threshold of the living' (Schwenk/Glatz 1982).

An organized system of ordering processes arises in a liquid when suitable physical conditions are offered. The formative laws inherent to the substance are suppressed through instabilities of the physical

| Stage | Form | Laws of substance |
|---|---|---|
| *Organism* | Species-specific, inherent, developing, foreign to substance | serve |
| *Mineral liquid* | Moving: organoid formation, unstable, unspecific, foreign to substance<br>At rest: amorphous, expansive, substance-neutral | |
| *Mineral solid*<br>Pseudomorphosis | Other-specific, determined by another substance | rule |
| Normal mineral | Permanent substance-specific crystalline or amorphous form | |

conditions: in pseudomorphosis during recrystallization, in the moving liquid through a whole range of flow instabilities. The various forces in play counterbalance one another in such a way that none of them is able to determine the course of events; thus other forces may intervene, controlling and deciding what will happen (see Jacobi 1998). This, incidentally, appears as a principle of modern chaos theory. Instability creates openings for other forces and provides opportunities for higher formative processes to intervene. For more than two decades, geophysicists and astrophysicists, for example, have spoken of the principle of shape formation by means of instabilities (Haerendel 1981, Shore 1992). It is well known that ordered structures do not come into being in nature until the conditions of their creation enter a phase of instability; instability being not the cause, but the prerequisite opportunity for formative processes to emerge. Steiner characterizes the suppression of one of the constituent members of a being (physical body, life-body, soul-body) by instability as a precondition for the intervention and triumph of the being's next higher constituent member (Steiner/Wegman 1925).

At the level of organic formation, it is not the substance's own formative force that act. The substance comes under the rule of the higher organic formative forces — and escapes them when it is excreted. The organic form is not a permanent state; it is being created at every moment in an ongoing process. Living organisms are in a continuous process of becoming, ceaselessly transforming what is achieved.

Thus, what we have to look at when considering life contexts is not the *substance's* own formative forces — that would refer to the level of the inorganic world — but its suitability to be seized and moulded by organic formative processes.

Picture-creating methods aim to reveal something of the life context of the substances under investigation. Because their samples are always and exclusively formless liquids, they exploit the higher organic, non-substance-specific formative paths open to the liquid state. They use instabilities in the liquid phase to arrive at the image, and to that extent differentiate themselves from substance-bound formative processes. The 'formative urge in matter' (Runge 1855) finds its limits precisely where Runge originally located it.

Understood in this way, picture-creating methods pursue the question of the type of *receptiveness* or *openness* that these liquids have for the higher formative forces, when the liquid sample is subjected to appropriate conditions. The purpose of picture-creating experiments is to create these conditions. For all their differences, the experimental set-ups are all arranged so as to open up the transition from the formless liquid to the form of the image by means of instabilities. Representative examples of this approach include Pfeiffer's sensitive crystallization, Kolisko's capillary dynamolysis, and Schwenk's drop picture method.

In the drop picture method, pure flow movements within a thin layer of liquid engender the forms, and the whole process takes place and remains in the liquid phase. The material passes through a huge range of flow instabilities, from the impact of the drop to the almost complete standstill of the resulting vortices. The transience of the flow patterns, which appear only as patterns of *movement,* is bridged using photography.

In capillary dynamolysis the liquid climbs against gravity up the capillaries of the filter paper. In the interactions between adhesion to the enormous surfaces of the capillaries (Harsch and Bussemas 1985), gravity, and evaporation — overlaid by reduction, oxidation, and deposition processes involving the composition of substances and the auxiliary metal salts used as aids — the material passes through a huge range of instabilities. Processes of climbing and swelling, concentrating and depositing intertwine and shape the resulting form according to the respective strength of their influence (Mandera 1995). When they dry out, the substances pass from the liquid to the amorphous solid state; the traces of their movement and precipitation appear as a lasting image.

For the processes involved in sensitive crystallization there is also a range of known instabilities, which initiate the formation and arrangement of crystals when the copper chloride solution becomes supersaturated (Barth 2003). Here we have a transition from the liquid state to a permanent solid, crystallized state, and it is primarily the arrangement of the crystals — and only in the second place their own form — that shapes the image; as in the organic world it is the arrangement of the substances, their complex interrelationships, that define the configuration.

So by observing nature, we can encircle and narrow down the physical conditions under which opportunities arise for a higher organic order to emerge, but this still leaves open the formative process itself. It demands investigation by spiritual science and is described in those terms by Rudolf Steiner (1922a).

Steiner describes liquid, and in particular water, as the bearer and mediator of the etheric in the physical world. In other words, the etheric is not part of the liquid, the liquid merely carries it. In the living organism — with its own etheric body — the liquid organism is the bearer and instrument of the etheric body. Liquids outside an organism are not influenced by an individual etheric body; they are touched by the etheric of the surroundings (Steiner 1924). As long as the liquids are opened up to the etheric by instabilities, the etheric can immerse itself in them, seize them, and initiate temporary formative processes in them. What we see here for the specific case of the liquid, Steiner also describes in a more general form (Steiner 1894, Steiner 1922b, Steiner/Wegman 1925, Schwenk 2000/2001).

First published in German as 'Die Rolle der Stoffe bei den Gestaltungsprozessen in der Natur und bei den bildschaffenden Methoden,' in: *Elemente der Naturwissenschaft*, Dornach, 2004. Translated by Nina Hausmann.

Wolfram Schwenk

# 12. Summary

Water responds to the tiniest of impulses with movement. To the extent that one can say: water is substance become movement. (E.A. Müller, Foreword in Wilkens *et al.* 2000)

Based on the comprehensiveness of our experience with the drop picture method, the following is a series of summary propositions of what appear to us to be the most important and relevant results of our research:

Liquid water is a material continuum. It behaves like a single entity, not like a substance composed out of sub-components. It reacts to influences and external stimuli in its entirety as a system, not in selective partiality.

Through movement, creative processes are stimulated in formless and passive water, processes which follow organic and cosmic natural laws. Through movement, water is opened up to the creative energies of living nature.

The ability of fluid water to creatively form and transform in harmonious flow shapes is considered an expression of its life-giving force and regenerative function in organisms.

What has become permanent shape and bonded substance in a solid body takes place in water as a formative development process. And crucially, in water, it remains on the process level.

These creative processes occur in water only while the water is moving; without movement they die away. This tendency of the flow forms to die away can be delayed by the addition of a viscous substance.

Differentiations in the creative movements of flowing water can be captured in images. By testing different water samples, the drop picture method can provide comparative depictions of these flow form differences. As an image method, the drop picture method lays open the latent potential of apparently formless water for form-shaping behaviour and is able to record this visually.

Carried out under standardized conditions, the drop picture method allows water the opportunity to show its creative flow patterns: Drops of distilled water are released at five second intervals into a thin layer of the still water sample within a petri-dish, stimulating water movement. These water movement patterns are made visible by a schlieren optical projector and then photographed.

The drop picture method uses the sensitivity and impressionability of the water's movement interfaces created during the water flow, during moments of instability.

Instability is essential to the generation of these creative water flow processes. The testing methodology consciously manufactures the necessary conditions of instability.

The drop picture method shows that the varying capacity for movement of different water samples reveals differences in their nature, and gives a holistic impression of each water sample's character.

The exact composition of any chemical substances present in the water cannot be identified by the drop picture method. The water flow is affected by the total interplay of the physical properties of the water sample — in particular density, viscosity, and surface tension in their mutual relationships. These are dependent as much on the level of dilution as on the type of substance. Several simultaneously dissolved substances work together to the extent that the drop-generated images cannot show their single respective influences. The drop picture method does not replace chemical analysis. It can however be a useful indicator in signalling the weakening of the mobility of the water due to the presence of foreign substances.

Materials used in the storage, transportation and distribution of water as well as in water treatment can influence the inherent mobility of the water. This can be tested by the drop picture method.

The drop-generated images are not a replacement methodology for analytical results. The form-creating process of the water flow movement is viewed as an independent aspect of quality, being an indicator of the overall entity and behavioural properties of the water sample. It can be used to complement and further the results of hygienic-analytical testing.

The drop picture method does not show whether water is potable or not. It shows whether water which is classified as potable has the same flow movement capability as natural clean ground water, or to what extent it does not.

Drinking water from a natural, clean, uncontaminated groundwater source shows, thanks to its capacity for movement, a wealth of diverse and creative polymorphic flow form patterns. Drinking water from other sources, such as conventionally treated water originally extracted from a dirty river source, shows weak, less diverse flow form patterns.

The drop picture method allows the description of a model image of good, fresh water with a positive characterization — not just through the elimination of negative factors but with the help of the description of the character of the water movement.

The natural purity of water is a functional necessity of its role as a life mediator. The importance of this purity does not reside only in the hygienic necessity of absence of negative components.

In productive areas of natural water bodies, where a diverse species range predominates with active constructive processes, water moves in polymorphic and diversified flow patterns. In destructive areas, where a simple species spectrum predominates with biological breakdown processes, water flows monotonously and undifferentiated. This contrast indicates that life processes and water flow have a common signature.

In water bodies, the flow pattern gives a similar integrated picture of the current prevailing character of the water as biological indicators do, in reference to past influences.

Previous incidents of movement, such as intense stirring, can influence the water's later behaviour.

Water manifesting shape-rich flow patterns can show slightly different flow patterns during different planet constellations than at other times. Dirty water does not share this characteristic openness.

First published in German as   'Zusammenfassende Thesen,' in: W. Schwenk (Ed.), *Schritte zur positiven Charakterisierung des Wassers als Lebensvermittler.* Herrischried, 2001. Translated by Jessica Read.

# References

Barth, J.G. (2003) 'Physik der Kristallisation mit Zusätzen.' Lecture of February 12, 2003, in Dornach.

Böhme, G. & Böhme, H. (1996) *Feuer, Wasser, Erde, Luft. Eine Kulturgeschichte der Elemente.* Munich.

Cloos, Walther *The Living Earth.* Lanthorn Press, UK, 1977.

Delli Priscoli, J., J. Dooge & R. Llamas (2004) *Water and Ethics. Overview.* UNESCO International Hydrologic Programme and World Commission on the Ethics of Scientific Knowledge and Technology. Series on Water and Ethics, Essay 1. Paris.

Franke, U. & Schwoerbel, J. (1972) 'Hydrographie, Chemie und Nährstofffracht eines mit organischen Abwässern verunreinigten Gebirgsbaches.' In: *Arch. Hydrobiol. Suppl.* 42, pp.95–124.

Haerendel, G. (1981) 'Gestaltbildung durch Instabilität.' In: *Naturwiss. Rundschau* 34:157–60.

Harsch, G., & H.H. Bussemas (1985) *Bilder, die sich selber malen.* Cologne.

Henderson, L.J. (1913) *The fitness of the environment. An inquiry into the biological significance of the properties of water.*

Hinrichsen, K.V. (Ed.) (1990), *Humanembryologie. Lehrbuch und Atlas der vorgeburtlichen Entwicklung des Menschen.* Berlin, Heidelberg, New York.

Institute of Flow Sciences (2004) *A Flow Science Towards Understanding Water* (Herrischried, Germany).

Jacobi, M. (1998/2001) 'Instabilitäten.' In: *Sensibles Wasser* 6, pp.128–31. Herrischried.

Jahnke, D. (1993) 'Morphologische Unterscheidungsmerkmale für die Auswertung von Wasserqualitäts-Untersuchungen mit der Tropfenbildmethode.' In: *Sensibles Wasser* 2, 41–68. Herrischried.

Kipp, F.A. (1951) 'Das Wasser als Zeuge für die Priorität des Lebendigen.' In: *Sternkalender* 1952, pp.66–73, Dornach.

Legner, A. (Ed.) (1985): *Ornamenta Ecclesiae,* Vol.1. Cologne.

Mandera, R. (1995) 'Zur Metamorphose von Pflanzenorganen, Substanzqualitäten und Bildtypen im Steigbild.' In: *Tycho de Brahe-Jahrbuch für Goetheanismus,* 1995, pp.281–310, Niefern-Öschelbronn.

Mütherich, E. & K. Dachs (Eds.) (1987) *Regensburger Buchmalerei.* Munich.

Pedretti, C. (Ed.) (1983) *Leonardo da Vinci. Natur und Landschaft. Naturstudien an der königl. Bibliothek in Windsor Castle.* Stuttgart and Zürich.

Peter, H.M. (1994) 'Das Strömungsverhalten des Wassers in der biologischen Selbstreinigungsstrecke des Schwarzwaldbaches Mettma.' In: *Sensibles Wasser* 4, pp.1–160, Herrischried.

Pflugfelder, O. (1962) *Lehrbuch der Entwicklungsgeschichte und Entwicklungsphysiologie der Tiere*. Jena.

Raethjen, Paul (1953) *Dynamics of Cyclones*. Leipzig.

Rapp, D. & Schneider, P.E.M. (1974) 'Das Tropfenbild als Ausdruck harmonischer Strömungen in dünnen Schichten.' Max-Planck-Institut für Strömungsforschung, *Bericht* 102, Göttingen.

Reichardt W. & Simon, M. (1972) 'Die Mettma — ein Gebirgsbach als Brauereivorfluter. Mikrobiologische Untersuchungen entlang eines Abwasser-Substratgradienten.' In: *Arch Hydrobiol. Suppl.* 42, pp.125–38.

Roob, A. (1996) *Das Hermetische Museum. Alchemie und Mystik*. Cologne.

Runge, F.F. (1855) *Der Bildungstrieb der Stoffe*. Oranienburg. Cited in Harsch and Bussemas 1985.

Schiller, F. von (1795) *Letters on the Aesthetic Education of Man* (Letter 5). New York, 1909–15.

Schneider, P.E.M. (1976) 'Sechs Instabilitätsphasen eines Ringwirbels als Grundlage für eine Klassifikation der Schwenk'schen Tropfbilder.' Max-Planck-Institut für Strömungsforschung Göttingen, *Bericht* 9.

Schnorr, J. (Ed.) (1978) *Beiträge zum Ausbildungsgang in der Tropfbildmethode*. Cultura Korrespondenz, Cultura Institut, Dornach.

Schreiber, I. (1975) 'Biologische Gewässerbeurteilung der Mettma anhand des Makrozoobenthos: Methodenvergleich.' In: *Arch. Hydrobiol. Suppl.* 47, pp.432–57.

Schmauss, August (1945) 'Biologische Gedanken in der Meteorologie.' In: *Forschungen und Fortschritte*, Vol. 21, No. 1–6.

Schwenk, T. (1950) 'Irdische und kosmische Eigenschaften des Wassers.' In: *Sternkalender* 1951, pp.65–69, Dornach.

—, (1962) *Das Sensible Chaos. Strömendes Formenschaffen in Wasser und Luft*. Stuttgart, Germany; translated as *Sensitive Chaos*, London 1996/2005.

—, (1967) *Bewegungsformen des Wassers*. Stuttgart.

—, (1985) 'Vom Wärmeorganismus der Erde.' (Lecture of 1974). *Sensibles Wasser* 1, pp.29–40, Herrischried.

—, (1988) *The Basis of Potentization Research*. Mercury Press, Spring Valley, NY.

—, & W. Schwenk (1989) *Water — The Element of Life*. Anthroposophic Press, Hudson, NY (USA). American edition of eight lectures by Theodor Schwenk, from 1967–79, and of four articles by Wolfram Schwenk from 1976–82, referring to their water research and the drop picture method.

Schwenk, W. (1998) *Das Wasser als lebenvermittelndes Element.* Ulm/D., Germany. Published in English as 'Water As a Life-Giving Element' in: A. Wilkens *et al.: Understanding Water.* 1st edn., Hudson, New York, 2002.

—, (Ed.) (2001a) 'Schritte zur positiven Charakterisierung des Wassers als Lebensvermittler. Ausgewählte Texte aus 40 Jahren Wasserforschung mit der Tropfbildmethode.' In: *Sensibles Wasser* 6, Herrischried.

—, (2001b) 'Wasser, das universelle Lebenselement.' In: *Sensibles Wasser* 6, pp.116–27, Herrischried; and in: *Elemente der Naturwissenschaft* 74, pp.8–25, Dornach 2001.

—, (2001c) 'Die Herausforderung einer wissenschaftlichen Annäherung an die "Lebendigkeit" des Wassers.' In: *WasserZeichen* No.13 (2000), pp.30–33, Herrischried; and in *Sensibles Wasser* 6, pp.150–52, Herrischried.

Schwoerbel, J. (1972) 'Falkauer Fließwasser-Untersuchungen an der Mettma.' In: *Arch Hydrobiol. Suppl.* 42, pp.91–94.

Selawry, Alla (1987) *Ehrenfried Pfeiffer. Pionier spiritueller Forschung und Praxis.* Dornach.

Shore, S.N. (1992) *An Introduction to Astrophysical Hydrodynamics.* San Diego.

Smith, H. (1974) 'A study of some of the parameters involved in the Drop picture Method.' Max-Planck-Institut für Strömungsforschung Göttingen, *Bericht* 111.

—, (1975) 'The Hydrodynamic and Physico-chemical basis of the Drop picture Method.' Max-Planck-Institut für Strömungsforschung Göttingen, Germany, *Bericht* 8.

Sonder, G. (1991) 'Der Wirbelexponent als Parameter kosmischer und zentrischer Wirbelarten.' In: *Elemente der Naturwissenschaft* 54, No.1, pp.82–100.

Steiner, Rudolf, 1894 (Complete Works (GA) 4) *The Philosophy of Freedom,* (Chapters 9 and 12), Rudolf Steiner Press, Forest Row 1999.

—, 1904/1922 (GA 9) *Theosophy, An Introduction to the Spiritual Processes in Human Life and in the Cosmos,* (Chapter 4), SteinerBooks, New York 1994.

—, 1916 (GA 272), *Geisteswissenschaftliche Erläuterungen zu Goethes Faust I,* lecture of September 11, 1916.

—, 1920 (GA 321), *Warmth Course,* lecture of February 2, 1924, Mercury Press, NY 2007.

—, 1921 (GA 205), *Therapeutic Insights, Earthly and Cosmic Laws,* lecture of June 24, 1921, Mercury Press, NY 2007.

—, 1921b (GA 323), *Das Verhältnis der verschiedenen naturwissenschaftliche Gebiete zur Astronomie.*

—, 1922a (GA 82), *Damit der Mensch ganz Mensch werde,* lecture & discussion April 8 and 9, 1922, Dornach 1994.

—, 1922b (GA 219), in Friedrich Benesch & Rudolf Steiner, *Reverse Ritual, Spiritual Knowledge Is True Communion,* lecture of December 31, 1922, SteinerBooks, NY 2001.

—, 1923 (GA 230), *Harmony of the Creative Word,* lecture of November 4, 1923, Rudolf Steiner Press, FR 2001.

—, 1924 (GA 234), *Anthroposophy and the Inner Life, An Esoteric Introduction,* lectures of February 1 and 2, 1924, Rudolf Steiner Press, FR 1992.

—, 1924/25 (GA 26) *Anthroposophical Leading Thoughts,* Rudolf Steiner Press, FR 1998.

— & Ita Wegman,1925 (GA 27) *Extending Practical Medicine, Fundamental Principles Based on the Science of the Spirit,* (Chapters 1–5), Rudolf Steiner Press, FR 1996.

Wachsmuth, Guenther (1932) *Etheric Formative Forces in Cosmos, Earth and Man: The Path of Investigation into the World of the Living,* Vol.1, 2nd ed., Anthroposophic Press, New York.

Wilkens, A. (2001) 'Polare Phänomene in Tropfbildströmungen.' In: *Sensibles Wasser* 7, p.40, Herrischried.

—, (2002) 'Druck und Sog, Polare Strömungen und Gestaltbildungen bei der Tropfbildmethode' In: *WasserZeichen* 17, p.22.

—, M. Jacobi & W. Schwenk (1995) *Wasser verstehen lernen.* Herrischried; translated into English as *Understanding Water.* Edinburgh 2005.

—, M. Jacobi, and W. Schwenk. (2000) 'Die Versuchstechnik der Tropfbildmethode: Dokumentation und Anleitung.' In: *Sensibles Wasser* 5. Herrischried.

Institute of Flow Sciences
Stutzhofweg 11
79737 Herrischried, Germany
www.stroemungsinstitut.de

# Index